kitten
training
for kids

kitten
training
for kids

sarah whitehead

photography by jane burton

BARRON'S

First edition for the United States and Canada published in 2002 by Barron's Educational Series, Inc.

First published in 2002 under the title of
Kitten Training for Kids

All inquiries should be addressed to:
Barron's Educational Series, Inc.
250 Wireless Boulevard
Hauppauge, NY 11788
http://www.barronseduc.com

Library of Congress Catalog Card Number:
2001088820
International Standard Book Number:
0-7641-2039-5

Project Editor: Warren Lapworth
Design: Joanne Dovey
Four-Color Separation: Michael Parkinson

Printed and bound in China

9 8 7 6 5 4 3 2

Picture Acknowledgments
All photographs by Jane Burton and Kim Taylor/Warren Photographic.

Models
Jumaane Bant
Tom Batchelor
Marcia Blake
Fynn Clive
Suzanne Cookson
Alice, Mina, and Louisa Facey
James Foulsham
Jemma Gregory
Arabella Grinsted
Kathyrn, Emily, and Joseph Main
Ben Monks
Jennifer, Latasha and Laurrie Murphy
Catherine and Peter Richards
Jed Taylor
Ji Tong
Gemma and Adelle Tracey

a note for parents

This book has been written to encourage children of all ages to take an active part in training and caring for their new kitten as a part of the family. Children are often exceptionally good at communicating with animals and can develop many different skills, as well as valuing kindness and compassion through their interactions with pets. All the exercises in this book are designed to be fun and friendly for both child and kitten. However, children and pets should always be supervised when interacting. It is therefore recommended that adult and child read through the book together and that all training and care is done with adult supervision.

Particular areas of concern are detailed in this book's "Parental Guide" boxes. If you are concerned about your cat's behavior, especially with children, contact your veterinarian for advice and a referral to a feline behavior specialist.

table of contents

introduction

At last, the day has arrived when you get a new kitten! Given care, love and thought, your new pet should give you and your family years of affection, fun, and happiness.

Cats are the most amazing of creatures. A combination of both wild and domestic animal, watching and guiding this animal's development will be fascinating and help to shape the adult cat it will become. Owning and caring for pets in childhood increases understanding of others' needs in adulthood, and is one of the most valuable experiences a young person can have. Enjoy the time that your kitten is a small bundle of fluff, ready to explore the world — it won't last for long!

taming a wild animal

From the day you introduce a kitten into your home, you will be living with a pet that is both domestic and wild! Even though our cats love to cuddle up with us, curl up on our laps, and enjoy the food that we give them, given the chance they become lone hunters, perfectly capable of looking after themselves.

Our pet cats are probably descended from the African wild cat (the Latin name for this cat is *Felis sylvestris lybica*). African wild cats are similar in appearance to our domestic pets, with a tabby-style coat.

Although cats have been living with man for over 4,000 years, they have changed very little. While dogs have been bred to be huge or tiny, with different types of ears, eyes, and coats, cats have remained almost the same size,

your kitten's development compared to a human's

kitten 2–4 weeks
child 1–3 years

and only the color and length of their coats and small differences in their tail or head shape have occurred.

kitten 12–18 weeks
child 11–13 years

kitten 4–8 weeks
child 4–6 years

kitten 8–12 weeks
child 7–10 years

kitten 5–9 months
child 14–16 years

kitten 9–12 months
child 17–adult

kitten development

Kittens grow much more quickly than humans. In as little as six months, kittens can grow to their adult size. They can run, jump, hunt, and behave just like an adult cat, while human babies are unable to walk, talk, or even crawl. How amazing it would be if you were to grow so quickly!

birth to two weeks

Kittens are born tiny, blind, and deaf. They are unable to keep warm without snuggling up to their mother and litter-mates (brothers and sisters). They are totally dependent on their mother for survival, and cannot even go to the toilet without her help.

However, kittens do have some powerful abilities — this is obvious from just one look at the size of a kitten's nose compared to the rest of its face! Despite the fact that the kitten's sense of smell is not fully developed until it is three weeks old, she can smell her mother's saliva and follow the scent to find mother and her milk.

Right from birth, kittens can purr, and this is probably used to tell the mother when the kitten is feeding and content. Cats continue to purr throughout their lives, to let us know when they are happy.

female and male

A mother cat is called a "queen"; a father cat is called a "tom". "Tom" is also used to describe any male cat.

two to four weeks

Kittens cannot walk properly until they are about 17 days old. Although they try to drag themselves around before this time, if their mother wants to move them, she uses her mouth to pick them up by the scruff of the neck. Kittens automatically become still and limp while being carried.

Kittens' first set of teeth start to appear after about two weeks. By the time kittens are three or four weeks old, they can go to the toilet by themselves and start to learn to use a litter box by copying their mother.

Mother cats carry their kittens carefully by the scruff of the neck.

Kittens just love to play — and it helps to teach them about the world.

also start to bite each other in play, and they need to learn what hurts and what doesn't.

four to eight weeks

Kittens usually start to be weaned at four to five weeks of age. This is when they start to eat solid food instead of milk, and begin to become a little more independent. Kittens of this age can run and jump, leap and climb, and can balance very well. They are able to groom themselves and will often lick and groom their brothers and sisters, too.

At this stage, it is very important that kittens begin to learn about the world around them. They need to meet and mix with lots of different people and other animals, such as dogs, and need to experience things that they will see and hear when living as a pet. Kittens that don't see lots of different sights and aren't handled by lots of people at this age can be shy or nervous forever.

At seven to eight weeks, most kittens are independent enough to leave their mother and litter-mates. Purebred cats (also called pedigree cats) usually cannot leave their mother until they are 12 weeks old, so they need extra play and handling from many different people before they go to their new homes.

eight to twelve weeks

As soon as they arrive with their new owners, most kittens start to mark their new home as their territory. Cats usually do this by rubbing their cheeks against furniture, walls, and even people!

They also start to play with each other. To begin with, their games are slow and clumsy, but they soon begin pouncing on their mother's tail and ambushing each other. Kittens of between three and four weeks old

Right from birth, kittens can purr to tell their mother that they are content.

above: *Kittens are born blind and helpless, but they quickly grow and develop.*

below: *Your kitten will practice hunting — even if all she catches are toys!*

Until your kitten can go outside after getting all her required vaccinations, the indoor area of your home is her entire world. She will probably love exploring, and doors, cupboards, and even bags that are left open will seem like enticing new places to explore. This short period of time is great fun for owners and kittens alike. Although having a young kitten can be hard work, it is absolutely fascinating to watch her antics as she learns about the world.

Your kitten may have all the muscles of an adult cat now, but she will still need to practice to become good at judging height, speed, and distance, to jump up onto furniture and across gaps, dash through a closing door, and grab a toy. Most kittens spend a lot of time practicing how to stalk and chase in play, and they often include people in their games.

three to six months

When your kitten has reached three months of age, she will be able to fend for herself, and may want to wander further than your yard

Cats love exploring outside, where they can run, jump, and play.

to explore. Cats have a very good sense of direction, so don't worry that the kitten won't be able to find her way home. She will also mark territory by spraying urine for other cats to find, which she can also use to find home.

Your kitten will reach maturity at around six months of age. This is the time to have your kitten neutered by the veterinarian, to prevent unwanted litters of kittens.

Your kitten should have settled into your household and be an accepted and loved member of the family. She should be confident with all the members of your household and your friends, and love to play at any

opportunity. Training is easiest while your cat is young, so teach her to come when called, and maybe even try to teach tricks.

six to twelve months

Your kitten is now a fully fledged cat. Most adult cats seem quite lazy, resting for many hours every day, but they are usually most active at dawn and dusk. Make sure that you play with your adult cat as often as you can. Throughout their lives, most cats enjoy the fun of a game of chase with a toy or the chance to "hunt" a length of string, proving that even though they are grown-up on the outside, inside there is a little kitten waiting to play!

how your kitten works
1 senses of smell and taste

smell

Kittens are born blind and deaf, but from their first moments they can detect smell, and soon recognize the smell of their mother's saliva, as she washes them all over by licking each kitten in turn.

A cat's ability to detect scent is perhaps the most important sense, after sight. This is because cats are designed to communicate with each other at a distance. In the wild, cats live alone. They only meet up to breed, or if there is a large amount of food they can share, then they go their separate ways again. The rest of the time, cats live by

themselves, and leave messages for each other using scent.

Individual messages are carried by scent in cats' urine, and in scent glands located all over the cat's body — particularly between the toes and in the cheeks. This means that when a cat rubs up against a tree, furniture, or you, she leaves a little of her individual smell behind! Humans cannot smell it, but other cats can — and they can gather information about the cat that left it, without ever meeting!

Cats that live together and are friends usually maintain their friendship by rubbing each other, sleeping together, and washing each other. This is known as "scent exchange" — both cats will want to mingle their scents as much as possible so that they both smell the same. You may find that your kitten does this to you, your family, and even other pets, to establish a "clan odor" — a smell that is shared by all members of the family. This makes her feel secure and comfortable, so you should encourage your kitten to rub on you and around the home as much as possible.

Cats also use their sense of smell to hunt down prey, and to find their way around when they are outdoors.

Cats' noses are incredibly sensitive, and scents are a very important part of their lives.

Even young kittens have excellent senses of smell and taste.

how the nose works

Cats have a sensitive lining or membrane inside the nose. Tiny scent particles in the air are dissolved by the moisture on the nose and inside the mouth, and then absorbed onto the surface of the membrane. The information from the membrane is recognized by a special part of the cat's brain, which allows it to gain information from the smell.

scent disguise

Cats recognize each other, and us, far more by smell than by sight. If you suddenly smell different, your cat may not know who you are for a little while! Strong deodorants and perfumes hide your own body smell, and when you return home your cat may want to sniff the scents you accidentally collected on your journey. Your cat will probably rub her cheeks on you so you smell like part of the family once again.

taste

We do not know much about cats' ability to taste food — mainly because we cannot ask them! Some cats are very choosy and only eat certain kinds of foods, whereas others will try almost anything and sometimes eat the most surprising things, such as wool or rubber! Cats are thought to be able to taste salt, bitter and acid flavors. However, their ability to taste sweet flavors seems very poor.

No one knows what food tastes likes to a cat, but this one is enjoying it! Cats are often very choosy over their food, so you will probably need to experiment to find cat food your kitten really likes.

2 sense of sight

Kittens are born completely blind, with their eyes tightly shut. It takes seven to ten days for them to start to open, and when they do the kitten probably cannot see clearly for some time. All kittens are born with blue eyes, but in time the color usually changes to become yellow, green, or orange, depending on the breed.

A cat's eye is very cleverly designed. Cats cannot see as much detail as we can, but they can spot even the tiniest movement from a great distance away.

Cats can also see much better than us in half-light. This is because they are designed to hunt their prey at dusk and dawn, when the light is failing or still brightening. Their eyes are shaped and constructed to collect the maximum amount of light available — they can see in light six times dimmer than humans can.

The cat's pupil — the black oval in the center of the eye that lets light inside — is very distinctive. During darkness the pupils

It takes seven to ten days for kittens' eyes to open fully, but their eyesight develops to be much better than ours.

automatically open wide, allowing lots of light to enter the eyes; in bright conditions, they close to narrow slits to prevent too much light entering the eyes. The pupils also change shape depending on the cat's mood!

the third eyelid

Unlike humans, cats have an extra eyelid. This thin fold of skin is not usually visible, but can be drawn across the eye horizontally, under the main eyelids. The only times that the third eyelid is obvious is when the cat is ill, and is a good indication that the cat needs veterinary attention.

how the eye works

The eye is a liquid-filled globe. It is set in a
bony socket in the skull and protected by pads
of fat and strong muscles, which allow the eye
to move around. The cat has eyelids, just like
us, which close if the whiskers or eye lashes
are touched, and which blink to keep the eye
moist. Blinking is also used in feline
communication.

At the back of the eye is a special layer of
cells, called the *tapetum lucidum*. This layer acts
like a mirror and reflects light shining directly
into the eyes, so they seem to glow when
caught in the beam of a flashlight or
automobile headlights. This natural effect led
to the invention of "cat's eyes" — reflective
objects that mark road lanes and help drivers
to find their way in the dark.

For many years, it was thought that cats
could only see in black and white. However,
recent research has shown they can distinguish
between red, blue, and white, although it is
thought they have trouble seeing shades of
red, and yellow and green look very similar
to them.

*Cats' eyes reflect
light, helping them
to see in the dark.*

3 sense of hearing

Just looking at a cat's constantly pricked ears shows how sensitive feline hearing is. Cats use their hearing to detect prey and can locate rodents underground by listening to their ultrasonic squeaks, sounds that humans cannot even begin to imagine.

Newborn kittens can barely hear at all, but this soon changes. They can locate their mother and litter-mates by the sounds of their purring and their meows.

Cats can hear a very wide range of sounds. They can hear much higher pitches than

unique ears

There is only one breed of cat that has significantly different-shaped ears to all the rest: the Scottish Fold. This unusual cat has ears that are tightly folded forward, rather than upward-pointing, like all other breeds. This feature does not seem to affect the cat's ability to hear.

humans and even dogs can (anything up to 1.5 octaves above the limit of human hearing). At lower levels, their hearing is probably similar to ours, but they are much better at locating the source of a sound.

You will be able to tell just how good your kitten's hearing is after she has become used to your routine. Just try opening a can or packet of cat food without your kitten hearing it — unless the cat is fast asleep, it's almost impossible!

Cats can move their outer ears in a variety of ways. They can prick them both forward together, turn one independently of the other, and flatten them both to their head. These ear

These Devon Rex kittens have huge ears and pixie-like faces!

above: *Ears pointed forward, this cat is alert.*

below: *Some all-white cats may be born deaf.*

how the ear works

The part of the ear that we can see is called the pinna, or ear flap. This is designed to funnel sounds down the external canal to the ear drum, which is well protected by the skull. Sounds of different pitch and different volume cause different vibrations of the ear drum, which passes the signal to the middle ear. This chamber houses three small bones that which act like a system of levers, sending vibrations to the inner ear, which are then converted into signals for the brain to recognize.

positions say more about a cat's mood than her ability to hear.

Some cats are born deaf. This is particularly likely in all-white cats, particularly if they have blue eyes. Other cats become deaf in old age, but deaf cats seem to manage well, despite their disability, and learn to rely on their other senses. However, care must be taken with deaf cats that are allowed outdoors, since they are particularly vulnerable to traffic accidents.

4 touch, warmth, and keeping cool

Perhaps the most sensitive parts of a cat's body are those areas that are not covered with hair: the paw pads and nose. The cat's nose is very responsive to warmth and to touch, and the paws are often used for exploring new objects: one paw is gently extended to pat the item, then the nose sniffs it.

the cat's whiskers

A cat's whiskers are the long, stiff hairs on either side of her nose. She uses them like an extension of her face, allowing the cat to feel things before touching them with her body. Whiskers are particularly useful in darkness, where the cat may use her whiskers to feel her way along if it's too dark see properly.

The rest of the cat's body is also responsive to touch, as you will know from stroking your kitten. Where your cat likes to be touched is very individual, but most don't enjoy being touched on the most sensitive areas, such as the nose or paws, so these places are best avoided.

You will be able to tell where your kitten

Kittens need to huddle together to keep warm.

likes being stroked by her response to your touch. Does she move closer to you and purr? If so, she's enjoying it! Does she move away or even use her paws to push you away? Find another area to touch.

temperature

Cats are sensitive to warmth and cold, and as any owner will tell you, they love warm places. Cats usually find the best spot in the home to curl up in warmth — even if that means stealing the best chair! However,

Cats' whiskers are very sensitive — your kitten probably won't like you touching hers.

sunburn

Some cats — especially white ones — need a little help from their owners in hot weather, as they can get sunburn on the tips of their ears and their nose. This can lead to serious illness, so it is important to put sunblock on your cat's nose and ears if they are normally white or pink, before she sunbathes.

hairless cats

Cats' coats vary a great deal — the length and style of coat is one of the main differences between breeds of cats. Cats can be long-coated or short-coated, but one exceptional breed has no coat at all! This is the Sphynx cat developed from one kitten that was born hairless in 1966. Since then breeders have selected cats to create this naked breed, which needs protection from the cold in winter and protection from the effects of the sun in summer.

despite their love of home comforts, cats come to no harm in cold weather and can exercise in low temperatures, and even hunt successfully in snow.

Most cats hate rain and do not enjoy being wet, although there are one or two breeds that swim voluntarily, given the chance!

In hot climates, cats need to keep themselves cool. This is done by finding shady places to rest and stretching out. Cats can only sweat through the base of their feet, which means that a hot or frightened cat may leave sweaty footprints behind!

A cat also keeps cool by panting and licking her coat all over. The saliva evaporates, cooling the body down.

above: *Cats pant to keep cool in very hot weather.*

below: *The Turkish Van cat breed loves swimming!*

5 movement and balance

Cats are elegant, muscular, and strong. Their bodies are perfectly designed as hunting machines, built to run, jump, climb, and pounce with speed and accuracy.

jumping

Cats are well designed to leap and can jump up to five times their own height. Just watching your kitten at home will show you how well cats can jump.

First, cats look up or across to the place they want to reach, calculating the distance and the angle of the jump they will need to make. Then they leap, like an athlete, landing easily and safely on their target — no matter how narrow.

However, coming down again is another matter. Most cats attempt to shorten the distance when jumping down, by edging their front feet down as far as possible and then springing off with their back legs.

Despite being designed as athletic hunters,

above: *The athletic cat in full leap.*

right: *Cats are excellent climbers — birds, watch out!*

cats are pretty lazy most of the time! They tend to walk rather than run, and sleep for anything up to 23 hours a day to conserve energy.

climbing

Cats can climb well, and often use their claws to help them grip the surface of the tree or fence as they climb. Fabrics are often favorites for this activity and kittens sometimes climb the drapes or furniture just for fun. Try not to laugh or encourage this at the start, as the kitten will grow and the furniture will suffer!

Occasionally, cats get stuck in trees or up telephone poles. Owners sometimes have to rescue their cats from these situations, but wait before helping your pet. Some cats seem to find the whole scenario rather funny and enjoy getting their owners to "save" them, when all along they could easily climb down themselves!

claws

Cats' claws are remarkable things, as they can be pulled back into the foot at will. This is called "retracting" and saves the claws from damage while a cat is walking or sleeping. The claws can be instantly extended if the cat needs them for climbing or holding onto prey. This explains how cats can be so gentle when they use their feet to play with us, yet use sharp claws to catch mice.

falling

Cats have an amazing ability to right themselves when they fall, to insure that they land on their feet. They automatically roll in mid-air while they fall, first to turn the head right side up, then allowing the body to follow. At the instant she lands, the cat arches her back to cushion the impact.

While this "righting reflex" is an amazing safety feature that all cats have, it does not prevent cats from being killed or seriously injured if they fall from a great height. It's very important to make sure that your kitten cannot fall from an upstairs window or from a balcony. Putting up a net or using safety latches on windows is sensible if you live in an apartment higher than the first floor.

The righting reflex means a cat should always land on her feet after a fall.

what your kitten needs

All kittens have basic needs. Just like us, they need food, water, health care, and shelter if they are to grow strong and stay well.

vaccinate your kitten by giving him a series of injections in the back of the neck or rear leg, which shouldn't hurt him.

Your kitten also needs to be taken to a

food and water

To begin with, give your kitten the same type of food that your kitten's breeder (or the mother's owner) has been giving him. This will insure that he won't have an upset stomach in his new home.

Make sure that your kitten has access to fresh drinking water, and that he knows where the water bowl is. Change the water every day to keep it fresh.

vaccinations and illness

Kittens need vaccinations to protect them from various diseases before they go out into the big, wide world. A veterinarian will

above: *Your kitten should have his own food and water bowls.*

below: *Vaccinations are very important.*

If your kitten is unwell take him to the veterinarian for an examination immediately.

keep things tidy

There are lots of things in your home that could accidentally make your kitten ill. To a kitten, headache tablets, cleaning materials, and even cassette tape can seem fun to play with, but can cause serious illness or even death. Keep all of your belongings, especially medicines, locked out of reach of your kitten to avoid accidents.

how to know if your kitten is ill

- Your kitten does not want to eat
- He has an upset stomach or throws up
- Your kitten visits the litter box more than normal
- He drinks more than normal
- Your kitten is tired, and does not want to move or play
- He does not groom himself
- Your kitten shows a third eyelid (*page 14*)

veterinarian when he is ill. The veterinarian will examine him, just like a human doctor checks your symptoms when you are ill, and give him treatment or show you how to care for the kitten so that he gets better.

If your kitten is unwell, be extra gentle with him. You might find that he doesn't want to play or is not interested in food or toys. If you think that your kitten is ill, take him to the veterinarian as soon as possible, especially if he has not eaten anything for a day or is drinking lots of water.

kitten needs checklist

- ❑ Food and food bowls
- ❑ Water and water bowl
- ❑ Soft brush
- ❑ Bed or cardboard box with blanket
- ❑ Traveling crate
- ❑ Litter and litter box
- ❑ Loving owner!

Make sure your kitten has his own bowl, set in a quiet part of the house.

A soft and cozy bed gives your kitten a special place of his own.

buy it. Cats love to hide and curl up when they sleep, so look for beds that have a small entrance hole at the front, like an igloo.

Cat cradles are also favorites. These fleecy beds are hung over the top of a radiator, so your kitten is kept deliciously warm while he sleeps!

beds

It is a good idea to provide your kitten with a bed of his own. This will help him to feel secure in the first few nights away from his first family.

Beds come in lots of different styles and fabrics. A cardboard box is okay at first, but cats prefer to snuggle into soft material, so line it with layers of cozy blankets or even an old sweater.

If you are going to buy a bed for your kitten, make sure it's one that is easily cleaned. Many cat beds can be cleaned in a washing machine, but check for this feature when you

The blissful warmth of a radiator cradle!

litter box

Even if you are going to allow your cat outside eventually, you will need to keep him in the home until he has had all his vaccinations, so you will also need to provide him with a place to go to the toilet. Most cats are very clean and will automatically use their litter box, as long as they know where it is and can reach it.

Litter boxes come in a variety of sizes and designs. The pan needs to be quite large, even for a small kitten, so that he can scratch around in it. Some have sides and a lid, with a flap at the front, which gives your kitten privacy and prevents the litter from being scattered around the room.

Litter should be fine-grained and natural; most cats prefer fine clay particles, or a special type of clay called fuller's earth, to man-made products. All cats like their toilet to be clean, so remove used litter several times a day, if possible.

toys and play

All kittens love to play, and this is an essential part of your friendship with your pet. Try to spend some time every day playing with your kitten. Find out what kind of toys he likes best (*see pages 52–53*) and have fun with him. Make sure that the games you play are safe, since kittens quickly grow into cats with big, sharp claws and strong teeth!

traveling

Your kitten will need to get used to traveling in automobiles, so that you can take him to the veterinarian. For safety, cats should travel in a carrying basket or crate. It is not safe to simply hold your kitten in your arms, since a frightened cat can easily leap away from you and run off.

Most cats dislike automobile travel for one reason only: they are usually being taken to the veterinarian! When most cats see the carrying crate and go in the car, they think something frightening is about to happen.

To help your kitten overcome this fear, leave the traveling crate or basket out in your home, so that it becomes part of everyday life. Play with your kitten in and around it and allow him to rub himself on it — that way it will smell familiar, too. If you do this regularly, you will be amazed at how easily your kitten will go in the traveling crate. You may even find that he enjoys travelling with you, instead of worrying about it.

above: *Kittens love to hide themselves away to rest.*

below: *A safe traveling basket is essential.*

going outside

If you are going to allow your kitten to go outside when he has had all his vaccinations, you may like to have a cat flap installed. These are specially designed cat doors, which they learn to use to go in and out of the home whenever they want. Most cats need to learn how to use a cat flap (*see page 64–65*).

It is important that other cats cannot get in through your kitten's door. If you live in an area where lots of other cats live, you might prefer a cat flap that is opened by a magnetic key on your pet's collar. This means that only your cat can open the flap to come into your home.

toilet training

Cats are naturally clean animals. They can be very choosy about where they go to the toilet, so it is sensible to try and make sure that everything you do is right for your kitten, to make her feel comfortable.

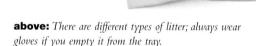

type of litter box

The most common type of litter box is an open plastic pan. This type is easy to clean, but some cats can make a mess around it by scratching up the litter and flicking it over the sides. Choose a box with a lid if your kitten makes a mess like this.

type of litter

Most cats prefer loose, rakeable litter in the tray. This is soft to stand on, forms into clumps, and is easy to clean up. Fuller's earth is a real favorite, although other clay-type litters are also popular.

Some litter contains scented particles or deodorizing material. Most cats don't like them, because they smell too strong for the sensitive feline nose and can irritate the pads of their feet.

how many boxes?

If your family has more than one cat, you will need more than one litter box, especially if all your cats live indoors all the time.

above: *There are different types of litter; always wear gloves if you empty it from the tray.*

opposite page: *Some cats prefer the privacy of a covered litter box.*

below: *Make sure your kitten's litter box is in a quiet place so she can use it without being interrupted.*

positioning the box

Think about this from your kitten's point of view. We don't want to eat our dinner in the bathroom, or have people around us while we use the bathroom, and cats are just the same.

Make sure the litter box is in a quiet place, well away from where you feed your kitten and away from where she sleeps. It is important that you kitten won't get ambushed while using the box — particularly by other cats or other pets, especially dogs!

cleaning the box

Your kitten's litter box should be kept very clean. Ask an adult to empty the box for you, or wear rubber gloves if you ever do this yourself. Always wash your hands afterward.

encouraging your kitten to use the litter box

If your kitten seems a unsure about using the litter box, you may need to encourage her at first. About once an hour, gently lift her into the box, and wait until the kitten uses it, then praise her gently and tell her how good she is. If your kitten doesn't go to the toilet, keep a close watch on her all the time until you put her in the litter box

again. Eventually, the kitten will go and use the box by herself, whenever she needs to.

If your kitten has an accident somewhere else in the home, do not punish her or shout at her. Cats can get so worried or anxious that they go to the toilet somewhere they shouldn't. Be patient with your kitten and ask advice from your veterinarian if it keeps happening.

Parental Guide

Provided that your kitten is kept in good health and is regularly de-wormed, she presents very little risk to human health in even the closest contact. However, pregnant women are strongly advised to avoid emptying litter boxes. If they must, they should wear rubber gloves when doing so, to avoid the slight risk of toxoplasmosis. Kittens and cats of all ages also love to use sand as a litter substrate, so children's sand boxes should be kept covered, or they might be used as giant litter boxes.

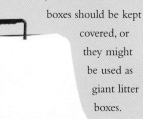

why does my kitten...?

crazy half-hours

● **Why do kittens do this?**

Some kittens have a crazy few minutes sometime in the day. The kitten will suddenly jump up with a strange expression on his face, and then dash around the room. Your kitten may prance around, using a strange side-stepping action, and arch his back. His tail will probably form an upside-down U shape and he may hold his ears right back.

● **What you need to do**

Although it may seem unusual to us, this behavior is perfectly normal for a kitten. Sometimes, it is linked to the time the kitten is fed. If your kitten goes crazy an hour or

With the back arched and side-stepping legs, this kitten is ready to run wild.

two after feeding, the food he is eating may not be right for him, and a different type of food could stop it from happening.

For some kittens, this wild behavior is simply a way to unleash lots of pent-up energy. In the wild, cats need to hunt for

Dashing around the room at full gallop uses up some of the energy a wild cat would use while hunting.

every meal and use up a lot of energy looking for and stalking prey. In our homes, there is no need for cats to do this, and you may find that your kitten tries to hunt you or the furniture instead!

This over-active behavior usually stops as soon as the kitten is allowed to go outside during the day, as he will get much more exercise and the opportunity to practice hunting — even if he isn't very good at it! Cats kept indoors are more likely to have crazy half-hours.

Occasionally, kittens learn that acting crazy leads to excitement from their owners, which can become an irritating, destructive, or even harmful habit. Kittens can learn that dashing around the room at top speed causes everyone to stop and look at them and laugh. Worse,

they may find that biting or scratching people as they run past brings even more excitement, screams, and squealing.

Unfortunately, if they get a big reaction to something they do, cats are likely to do it again. It may be funny to see a small kitten climbing the drapes or attacking your ankles, but think how this will feel when the cat is fully grown. If your kitten often gets over-excited, try to ignore him as much as you can, by getting up and walking out of the room. Don't say or do anything, but simply leave. He will soon learn that wild behavior is not as much fun without an audience.

chasing birds
● **Why do kittens chase birds?**

Cats are hunters. They are so good at it that even though we feed them and care for them in our homes, they instinctively want to chase fast-moving objects or animals. Some cats are so excited by this kind of chasing that they will stop eating their dinner to chase something. Your kitten isn't being unkind or cruel if he chases birds, or even catches them — it's simply what cats are designed to do.

Cats' incredible agility and flexibility is often shown in a crazy half-hour, but don't let your kitten's wild behavior get out of hand.

● What you need to do

If your kitten wants to chase things, try and get him interested in chasing toys that you can play with, too. Wand toys, with fluttering feathers tied on the end of a string, allow your cat to behave in a natural way, but without harming another creature. This may not stop your cat from chasing other things too, but at least some of his energy will be used safely.

Some owners attach a small bell to their cat's collar, to warn birds and small animals of their pet's approach. However, clever cats soon learn to stalk animals so carefully the bell stays silent!

bringing prey home

● Why do kittens bring prey home?

Cats that catch birds, mice, or even other, larger prey in the yard or beyond may bring it home to their owner as a gift! While we might not be pleased by this, the cat is only acting as nature intended.

Cats learn to catch small animals very early in life — and even kittens can be good hunters, if they have the opportunity. Bringing the poor victim home and

Cats can leap high into the air to catch birds — or wand toys!

left: *Cats are predators, designed to hunt, stalk, and chase.*

presenting it to you shows that your kitten regards you as a family member — he is trying to share food with you. Although humans find this unpleasant, don't be angry with your kitten, as he is only following his instinct to bring "prizes" back to the family den.

Some cats bring prey to their owners as "gifts" — an unpleasant but natural thing for them to do.

● What you need to do

Sometimes cats bring live animals into the home. It is not unusual for live mice to be brought in through the cat flap and dropped on the kitchen floor, to run around! If you love all animals, the only answer is to set a humane mouse trap — one which will not hurt the mouse when it is caught — then take the animal outside and release it again.

licking himself

● Why do kittens lick themselves?

Cats are very clean creatures and like to keep their skin and coat in top condition. They do this by grooming themselves frequently using their tongue and paws to act like hairbrushes.

The cat's tongue is cleverly designed for grooming. If a cat has ever licked your fingers, you will know how rough and raspy it feels. The surface of the tongue is covered in tiny bumps, and some are even shaped like

Every inch needs a wash! But if your kitten grooms himself too much, take him to the veterinarian.

right: A cat uses his rough tongue to clean himself, using a paw on those hard-to-reach places.

backward-facing hooks, which help to remove dead hair and pieces of dirt from the cat's coat.

The cat's tongue is very long and can groom almost every part of the cat's body, even if he has to get into strange positions to reach those awkward areas! The only parts the cat cannot reach with his tongue is the face and behind the ears. These areas are washed by licking the side of the paws and then rubbing them with the paws.

● What you need to do

Grooming is usually a good thing, but cats and kittens sometimes groom themselves to feel more secure. This is a little like us biting our fingernails when we are worried. Cats also seem to wash when they feel awkward. We have no idea if cats can feel embarrassed, but they behave like they do after they have made a mistake, such as falling off an obstacle that they were jumping onto, or after being frightened by something that they see every day.

If your cat grooms too much, so he loses some of his coat, take him to the veterinarian. There may be a physical reason, like fleas, or the kitten may be overly nervous and groom to calm himself.

dribbling and kneading
● Why do kittens dribble and knead?

When your kitten is settled in your home, he will start to regard you as his family. In your cat's eyes, you

covering food

Occasionally, a kitten tries to cover up leftover food by scratching the floor around his bowl. He is trying to hide the food, to keep it for later. Wild cats do this to prevent other animals from eating food they have caught. Our cats do not need to do this, but the behavior remains.

right: A very young kitten gets comfort from soft fabric, but his claws can damage furniture when he's older.

become his mother, providing food, security, warmth, and resting places.

Some kittens take this to heart and can behave as they would with a feline mother. If they are being cuddled and feel really content, they dribble in anticipation of nursing and may knead their owner with their front paws to encourage milk to be produced!

● **What you need to do**

Some owners find this behavior cute and enjoy the closeness that it brings. For others, the thought of their kitten dribbling on their shirt is unpleasant and they wish it wouldn't happen.

If your kitten becomes too much of a "baby," try playing more active games, rather than cuddling him.

scratching things
● **Why do kittens scratch?**

All cats need to scratch, and while most do this outdoors if they can, on tree trunks and posts, some scratch furniture, carpets, or even stairs.

Scratching has two main functions. Cat's claws are continually growing, so the outer layer or "sheath" of the claw comes loose and falls away. Scratching helps to remove the sheath.

Cats also scratch to leave scent messages. They have scent glands between the pads of their paws, and when they scratch on something, they leave behind an invisible message. The scent tells other cats that they have been there.

"Ouch!" It can hurt if a kitten or cat uses his claws when he kneads you.

● **What you need to do**

If you are keeping your kitten indoors, encourage him to use a scratching post. This should be at least as tall as the kitten when he stands on his hind legs and reaches up with his front paws. Don't forget that he is going to grow, so get a tall one, or be prepared to buy another post when your kitten is fully grown.

The post should be covered in sisal string or tree bark. Carpet is best avoided, as your kitten might think that it's okay to scratch on all kinds of carpet.

If your kitten prefers to scratch on the floor, find a piece of wood that you can lay out on the floor for him to use. Make sure the wood won't splinter into pieces when it is scratched — splinters can get stuck in cats' paws.

If your kitten scratches the furniture or carpet, distract him, then cover the area so he cannot immediately scratch it again. Make

watching TV

Your kitten might enjoy watching television. Although cats do not see in the way that people do, many like watching moving images on TV, especially birds or other animals that fly or make high-pitched sounds. Some cats are so convinced that the pictures are real that they go around to the back of the television set to see if they can find where the animals are coming from!

Video cassettes made specially for cats are on sale in many places. Designed to catch your cat's attention and keep him entertained, mice, birds, fish, and even moths appear on the screen. Special high-pitched sounds on the cassette are attractive to cats but not noisy for human ears.

sure that your cat is relaxed and content in the home — cats sometimes scratch to mark their territory if they are feeling nervous.

chasing his tail

● **Why do kittens chase their tails?**

Cats love to chase anything that moves. Kittens sometimes get excited when they see the end of their own tail waving around! They sometimes turn in circles to catch it, and then may play with it like a toy.

It's far better for kittens to sharpen their claws on a scratching post than on the furniture!

right: *Cats have fun chasing their tails but soon find it's better to play with toys and leaves.*

● What you need to do

Although this behavior is funny to watch, do not give your kitten too much attention when he does it. Some cats learn to chase their tails just to get attention, and this can become annoying or even harmful if he bites his tail too hard.

digging in flower beds

● Why do kittens dig?

Because cats are so clean, they usually prefer to cover up the area where they have been to the toilet. Your kitten will probably dig a small hole, go to the toilet, then pull soil back over the area to hide it.

If a cat leaves the soiled area open and does not cover it, he is leaving a message for other cats that he has been there.

● What you need to do

If your cat keeps going to the toilet in the middle of your parents' favorite flower bed, use netting to keep him off it. Do not shout at the kitten or get angry if he goes in the wrong place, or he might stop going to the toilet outside.

arching the back

Most cats only arch their backs when they are frightened of something or when they are stretching. If your kitten is worried about something, he may arch his back right up, put his tail up in the air, and fluff out his coat to make himself look as big as possible. These efforts are designed to scare away the thing that frightened him. When the threat has gone away, he will calm down and his hair will become smooth again.

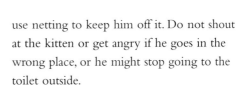

companionship, security, and respect

Although cats live by themselves in the wild, living as our pets they need love and companionship. Some cats are naturally affectionate, wanting to be with you all the time, and enjoying being petted and cuddled. Others seem more independent and like being alone outdoors. They might enjoy playing games with you or being outdoors with you, but they are less likely to want to be cuddled. Whichever type of kitten you own, it is important that you spend time with her to build your friendship.

Sometimes kittens get very attached to one person in the family, or to another cat or dog you may own. To make sure that your kitten enjoys being with you as much as with her furry friends, you will need to work extra hard and make sure that you spend time with all of the family pets separately. Spending time with your new kitten is exciting and fun to begin with, but as the kitten grows bigger and your

above: *A contented kitten.*

left: *Some cats love to be held and stroked, others prefer to play.*

Playful and adventurous; spend time with your kitten every day.

time is taken up with school and friends, she can become lonely and ignored. Cats need to be stroked, fed, and played with every day if they are to enjoy being with you. Try to spend time with your pets, even if it's only for a few minutes each day.

respect

All good friendships are based on respect. This means that you need to be kind to your kitten and understand that you do not always agree with each other. There may be times when you want to play but your kitten wants to sleep, or you may be concentrating on doing your homework when your kitten wants to play.

hand care

Your hands should always mean safety and pleasure to your kitten. Smacking your cat, or playing rough games where your kitten chases your hand and pounces on you, are inappropriate ways of interacting with your cat. Many owners of adolescent or adult cats regret having taught their pet to play these sorts of games, where their hands are the cat's "prey." These types of behavior can be amusing when the kitten is young, but are dangerous with a grown cat.

Remember that your kitten does not understand the words that you use, and be patient with her. If your kitten is annoying you, just put her out of the room and shut the door. It is very important that you never tease your kitten, pull her tail, or chase her. Smacking, shouting, pushing, or pulling may frighten her so never do these things to any cat.

If your cat seems to be in a bad mood, tell an adult. Just like us, cats have good days and bad ones, and they can't tell us if they're feeling unwell and just want to sleep.

Stroke kittens and cats gently and calmly.

socialization

Just imagine what people must look like to your kitten. We must seem like giants, with thundering voices, strange movements, and odd smells. It is easy to see why they might be scared of us. Cats need to learn about people, so that they are not frightened by them. They need to understand that people look different, smell different, and sound different from each other. Your kitten needs to become used to all sorts of people very early, or he may never be truly confident with humans.

Getting used to being with people of different sizes, ages, and appearances is called socialization. Your kitten needs to meet lots of people before he is too old to learn that we are not a threat. Kittens need to meet and be handled by as many people as possible between the ages of five and 12 weeks. This is very young and is normally before most owners even get their new kitten. This is why all kittens should come from a breeder who encourages as many people as possible to meet the kittens with their mother, before they go to their new homes.

Even if your kitten met lots of people before he came to live with you, and seems to be outgoing and bold, keep introducing him to different people. Try to think what new people might look like to a cat — a man with a beard, for example, must look very strange if your kitten has only met

above: *Play will increase your kitten's confidence.*

Introduce your kitten to your friends as soon as possible. The more people, the better!

women and children! A child wearing a hat or someone walking with a stick might look odd and scary.

Try to make sure that all of your visitors take time to meet your kitten and perhaps play with him or offer him a treat, then he will grow up knowing that all people are fun to be around.

if your kitten is frightened of people

Your kitten may have come from a breeder who did not introduce him to many people before he was six weeks old, or from a shelter where the number of people he saw was rather limited. If so, your kitten may be rather frightened of meeting new people, and may run away when visitors come to your home. He may even be frightened of you.

If your kitten is afraid of people, it is very important that he is not forced to meet them, but becomes used to humans in his own time. Do not try to follow him to stroke him or to pull the kitten out from a hiding place.

Use food and toys to help your kitten overcome his fears. If your kitten is afraid when your friends come to the house, ask them to play with him or feed him. Most kittens cannot resist the sight of a piece of string being dragged past their hiding place!

Wait until your kitten comes out, then ignore him. Don't try to stroke him immediately, but allow him time to watch the person and sniff them. He may even want to pretend that they are not there for a while, and this is okay too.

Only try to stroke a nervous cat when he chooses to come to you for petting, no matter how long it takes. When your kitten becomes more confident, invite more friends and he will get braver and braver.

Use food and toys to encourage your kitten to approach — don't follow him.

habituation

In the wild, a cat never meets strange things like washing machines, vacuum cleaners, or children! Your kitten needs to get used to all the sights, sounds, and smells in your home from the beginning, so that she is not afraid of them. This is called habituation.

Very young kittens show little fear of new objects, so this is the time to introduce them to as many different experiences as possible. Most kittens are only too eager to explore, so make sure that they are safe while they get used to your home and yard.

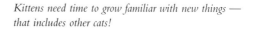

Kittens need time to grow familiar with new things — that includes other cats!

sights

From a kitten's point of view, some parts of our lives must look very strange. Imagine seeing someone wearing a crash helmet or seeing (and hearing!) someone using a hairdryer for the first time! It is not surprising that some kittens run away when see these unusual sights — it takes time for them to understand that they are not dangerous and can be ignored.

Introduce your kitten to new things and sights, smells, and sounds every day.

rewards for bravery

If your kitten is scared by something, try not to reassure her. Instead, wait until she is being brave, then stroke and make a fuss over her to praise her confident behavior.

sounds

Cats have extremely good hearing, so even soft sounds must seem a little loud and noisy to them. Kittens need to hear all the normal sounds in your home — people talking, television, the telephone ringing, music, and so on — over and over again, so that they become used to them.

smells

Cats have a very good sense of smell. They can identify people by their scent, and learn to recognize members of the family this way. Kittens need to be handled by lots of different people, family and friends, so they are not scared of unfamiliar people and their different scents and appearances (*see also pages 38–39*).

touch

Your kitten needs to learn that being touched is pleasant, not frightening, then she will enjoy being stroked by you and your family and friends. A kitten that is used to being touched is easier for the veterinarian to handle when your pet needs treatment.

Handle your kitten every day. Always make it a pleasant experience (*see page 42*).

safety first

Some kittens can get into trouble when they are exploring. Have a look around your home and yard from a cat's point of view. Can your kitten get into a shed or garage where she might get stuck or locked in?

Ponds should be covered with netting and rain barrels should have fitted lids. Cats can swim, but a kitten may not be able to get out of a deep pond or container and might drown if she became too tired.

Check to be sure that your kitten cannot reach any medicines, chemicals, or cleaning materials. Cats often find the smell and taste of poisonous substances attractive but become ill if they eat them.

Best friends! Cats can accept other types of animal as members of the family. Cats can even learn to get along with dogs, so long as their first meetings are kept under careful control.

handling your kitten

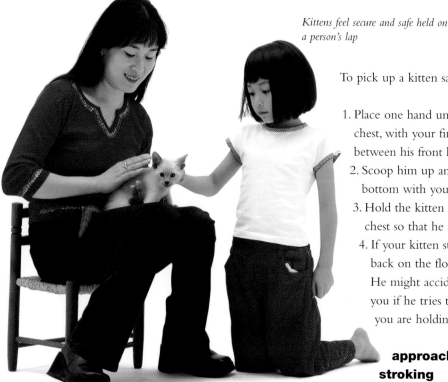

Kittens feel secure and safe held on a person's lap

To pick up a kitten safely:

1. Place one hand under the kitten's chest, with your fingers spread between his front legs.
2. Scoop him up and support his bottom with your other hand.
3. Hold the kitten close to your chest so that he feels safe.
4. If your kitten struggles, put him back on the floor immediately. He might accidentally scratch you if he tries to jump while you are holding him.

approaching and stroking

In "cat speak," it is bad manners to approach a cat and offer it attention! Cats like to be the ones who ask for attention, and feel much more comfortable if they are allowed to do this. Some cats will run away from you if they are feeling worried, and they feel worse if you follow them and try to make friends. Instead, sit quietly and wait for the cat to come and say hello.

As soon as he starts to move toward you, turn your body away slightly and narrow your eyes (*see pages 82–83*). Then you can offer your hand, and start to stroke the cat or kitten if he seems to want this.

There is nothing more enjoyable than sitting on a couch with your cat cuddled up next to you, purring softly! However, your kitten will only learn to enjoy your attention and affection if you handle him with care and respect.

picking up your kitten

Kittens need to feel secure when they are picked up and held. If you are worried about doing this, or have a very energetic, wriggly kitten that might try to jump from your arms, ask an adult to help.

Stroke the cat around the face and ears to begin with. The area behind the ears is often a cat's favorite place to be tickled. If he enjoys this, you can stroke along his body and up his tail. Always stroke in the direction of the hair and listen carefully — if the cat's purring, he's happy!

Not many cats enjoy having their stomach

try these ways of stroking to find out where your kitten likes being tickled:

1. Tickle the kitten around the back of his ears. Watch your kitten closely. If he enjoys this, he will purr and move closer to you.

2. Now stroke the back of his neck. Does he try to rub her chin on you? If so, he's enjoying the attention.

3. Try stroking your kitten from head to tail, along his back. Watch carefully to see where he likes being stroked the best, then choose that place when you want to give him attention.

Parental Guide

Dropping a kitten or holding it in a way that causes discomfort or distress can result in irreparable physical and emotional damage to the kitten and, potentially, to your child. Encourage your children to groom and examine the kitten on the floor, or, with your help, after carefully lifting him onto a non-slip surface.

or feet touched. Although some cats learn to roll over and be petted, this takes time and a trusting relationship with the owner. It is far better to start with places that your kitten enjoys being touched, and build your friendship from there.

When you are petting and stroking your kitten, try to be calm and quiet with him. Many cats will run away from sudden movements or noises, and even sneezing frightens some kittens.

holding your kitten

Kittens can scratch and even bite if they feel frightened when they are picked up. You need to be very careful and might need an adult's help.

Are you…?

up to 7 years old Do not try to pick up your kitten — ask an adult to do it for you

7 to 10 years old Only ever pick up your kitten with an adult to help you

10 to 14 years old Only pick up your kitten if you need to — follow the "safe holding" rules very carefully.

how to examine your kitten

Examining your kitten every day means you will be the first to notice if your kitten is not well, or if he has a cut or graze. Inspecting your kitten prepares him for being handled by strangers, particularly the veterinarian. If you have a toy stethoscope you can even listen to the cat's heart.

Inspect your kitten from head to toe

1. Support your kitten from underneath with one hand to keep him standing, or ask an adult to help you. Now look into each eye. Check that they are bright and clean.

2. Move onto your cat's ears. Lift the ear flap slightly and look down the ear canal. Talk to your kitten, and stroke him if he stays calm.

3. Now ask an adult to lift your kitten's lips, first one side, then the other, to allow you to look at both sides of his teeth. Then the adult should open the kitten's mouth very gently so you can see the tongue and throat. Praise and give a special food treat for good behavior.

4. Move on to the neck and shoulders. Feel every inch of the kitten's skin and coat, moving gently down the front of each leg. Lift the front feet one at a time to look at

Carefully check the eyes; never touch the eyeball itself.

Look into the ears and check that they are clean.

preventive healthcare

Preventive healthcare means giving your kitten medical treatment, such as a worming tablet or flea powder, so he won't catch a bug or disease.

Vaccinations

Kittens need to be vaccinated against diseases including feline leukemia, cat flu, feline enteritis, and chlamydia. Vaccinations will depend on where you live and whether the kitten is likely to be exposed to possible infection. Your veterinarian will give you advice.

Worming

Kittens should be regularly wormed against internal parasites, or worms. Worms vary from country to country and can even be dependent upon local geography. Get the worming medicine — tablets, granules, or liquid — from your veterinarian.

Flea protection

In an average lifetime of a few weeks, the female flea can lay over 2,000 eggs — if left untreated, a few fleas on a kitten can quickly

your kitten's claws, then tuck the paw under, to inspect the pads on the bottom of the foot.

5. Moving back up to the shoulders, run your hands down your kitten's coat to his hips and then down your cat's ribs. Can you feel them?

6. Feel down each hind or back leg, then inside the thighs. Lift and examine each rear foot, one at a time, as you did the front ones.

7. Finally, stroke down the whole of your kitten's body, from his head to the tip of his tail.

Be calm and very gentle while you are examining your kitten. Give him special food treats throughout for being good, and give some food or play a game with a toy when you are finished.

Look at the foot pads; the kitten may have damaged one.

An adult should open the mouth for you to check inside.

Examine the kitten's skin and coat.

develop into several thousand! While examining your kitten you might find fleas or black specks of "flea dirt." Your veterinarian can provide insecticide chemicals, in the form of shampoos, powders, and sprays, that kill fleas and flea eggs.

Neutering

The advantages of neutering your kitten can be discussed during your kitten's first veterinary check-up. Ask your veterinarian to check your kitten's gender —it can be quite embarrassing to find that your kitten shouldn't be called Tom because "he" is a girl, not a boy! Cats are usually neutered before they reach six months old.

Dental care

As they get older, many cats suffer from bad teeth and infected gums. Certain breeds are prone to very early gum disease and tooth decay. Daily handling of the head and mouth will make once-weekly tooth-brushing a lot easier (see page 48) and prevent dental problems.

grooming your kitten

Cats and kittens are very good at grooming themselves, but brushing your kitten will help her to become used to being handled and will make your friendship even stronger. Some cats, such as Persians and other longhaired varieties, manage all the grooming they have to do, and will be grateful if you help to keep them clean and stop their hair getting matted.

The sooner your kitten becomes used to being groomed, the easier it will be. It is important that your kitten enjoys being groomed, and that you do not accidentally pull

above: *Keep your kitten's eyes clean and the fur below them free of stains.*

her hair. A painful experience can make a kitten afraid of grooming for the rest of her life, so be very gentle. Ask an adult to help if your kitten won't keep still.

how to groom your kitten
Brushing

Hold your kitten gently on your lap or a table, and start by brushing along your kitten's back. Always brush in the direction that the hair grows.

Next brush her legs, head, belly, and then tail. Be gentle and watch your kitten carefully. Stop if you think that your kitten is becoming agitated or fearful, or tries to get away.

Be very gentle when using a comb, and talk calmly to reassure your kitten.

above and *right:* *If you are gentle, grooming should be an enjoyable experience for the kitten.*

Combing

Comb through the hair in the direction it grows. Be careful not to tug or pull.

If you find some matted hair, ask an adult to remove it with scissors, rather than risk hurting your kitten with the comb.

grooming equipment

Brushes: The type of brush you need depends upon your kitten's coat. A soft bristle brush is usually ideal. If your kitten has a short coat, a rubber brush can give her a massage while you groom.

Comb: A metal-tooth comb is ideal for removing dead hair. Make sure that the teeth have rounded ends that will not scratch the kitten's skin.

Velvet glove: These are ideal for putting a shine on smooth-coated cats. Most kittens really enjoy being stroked with one of these mitts.

Cotton balls: This is useful for wiping ears and eyes. Insure that you use a clean piece for each job.

Using a glove

You can now polish your cat so that she really shines! Use a velvet glove or mitt and simply stroke your cat from head to tail.

Cleaning ears

Cleaning your cat's ears shouldn't be necessary. If your kitten's ears look or smell dirty, she probably has an infection that needs treatment from the veterinarian, rather than simple cleaning.

The ear flap can be carefully wiped, but never poke anything into the ear.

right: *When your kitten is used to combs, brushes, and being handled, she will relax while being groomed.*

Never poke any object or cotton ball into the ear. The inside of the ear flap can be wiped gently with baby oil, or a dampened cotton ball.

Cleaning eyes

Some cats suffer from tear-staining under their eyes, which makes the hair look brown. This is particularly common in flatfaced breeds. Wipe under the eyes with a dampened cotton ball to remove some of the staining; you probably won't be able to clean the tear stains away completely.

cleaning teeth

If you are really committed to keeping your kitten in the best possible health, you will need to clean her teeth! Just like us, cats get tooth decay and gum disease if their teeth become dirty, but special cat toothpaste, and toothbrushes that fit on the end of your finger, can get them clean. This can be an awkward job and needs lots of patience and practice — you are sure to need an adult's help. Brush your cat's teeth once a week, if you can.

Your kitten will lose her baby teeth by the age of around five months. Check in your kitten's mouth every week. Make sure that your kitten's mouth looks clean and healthy and that her breath smells okay.

left: *Teeth-cleaning pads make this job a little easier.*

right: *Cats are experts at doing their own grooming.*

left: *Cats sometimes snag their collars on something, so make sure you use one she can slip out of.*

are gone.

To dry your kitten, gently wrap a towel around her, like a cocoon. Most cats dislike the sound and feeling of a hair dryer near them, so it is best to remove as much water as possible with the towel, and then keep your kitten warm until she is thoroughly dry.

putting on a collar

If your kitten is going to be allowed outside, it is sensible for her to wear a collar. This is so that she is easy to identify and can be returned to you if she were to become lost.

You must use a collar designed for cats. These have a special elastic safety feature, so if your kitten's collar gets caught on a branch or fence post, she can break free of the collar or pull her head out of it. Attach an identity tag, containing your name and address and phone number, to the collar.

Collars come in lots of different colors and designs. Some are made of reflective material, which makes your cat easy to spot at night.

bathing

It is rare for a cat to need a bath. However, occasionally one will roll in something smelly, or get oil on the coat, and then she will need help to get clean. Bathing a cat can be quite difficult — simply because not many cats like being wet, even if the water is warm. Ask an adult to help you and get all the necessary equipment ready before you start.

Bathing is best done in the bathroom or kitchen sink, using warm water and a special shampoo made for use on cats. An adult will need to hold your kitten firmly, while you pour the water over her coat. Lather her coat with diluted shampoo (shampoo weakened by adding water), then thoroughly rinse it with clean water till all traces of the shampoo

Most cats hate being bathed and will do anything they can to avoid getting wet... except for the Turkish Van (*page 19*)! These beautiful cats love to swim, and will jump into the tub and swim around whenever they get the chance. Some even learn to turn on taps, so they can take a shower!

giving attention

Your kitten will need lots of attention, particularly in the first few weeks and months of his life. However, *when* you give him attention is up to you.

Some cats learn naughty ways to get their owner's attention. They jump on their owners, scratch them, or even bite them! Others learn to climb the drapes, knock ornaments off a shelf, or howl in frustration when they want affection! All this might seem funny at first, but when it starts to happen at two o'clock in the morning, it's no laughing matter.

Make sure that you play with your kitten when it's convenient for you. If it isn't, ignore him altogether, until you have finished what you are doing.

Ignoring your kitten can be difficult. Cats can be very persistent, meowing all the time or jumping on an owner's lap no matter how often they are put back onto the floor. To ignore this sort of behavior you need to do some acting....

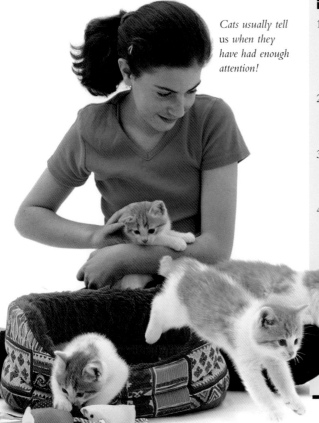

Cats usually tell us when they have had enough attention!

ignoring your kitten

1. If you need to ignore your kitten, make it very clear that you are not going to give in and give him attention, no matter what he does. First turn your back to the kitten.

2. Look away from your kitten, and fold your arms, to show that you are not going to play with him or give him any attention now.

3. Do not say anything to the kitten, and don't push him away or stroke him to keep him quiet.

4. If your kitten keeps trying to get your attention, get up and walk out of the room, shutting the door behind you, or ask an adult to put him in another room where he cannot disturb you.

When you are ready to play, you can give your kitten as much attention and affection as you want.

their owners in the middle of the night, and this can be a very difficult problem to solve if they are rewarded by strokes and attention.

If your cat wakes you during the night, think what he might need. Can he get to his litter box if he needs to go to the toilet? Is he hungry? Is he feeling unwell? If you know that he is fine and well fed and can reach his litter tray, try to ignore him.

If your kitten repeatedly tries to get attention, make him comfortable in another room for the night and leave him alone. It might be tempting to go to him if he cries or scratches for attention, but you will have to do this every night if you start the habit!

Your kitten needs attention and will enjoy being close with you, but waking you up or meowing for attention in the night or while you are busy needs to be ignored to insure that you all get time to do the things you want to — like sleep!

top left: *Some cats learn to demand attenton!*

below: *All kittens are curious, but some do naughty things just to get our attention.*

bedtime trouble

Most cats love to curl up at the foot of the bed and sleep with their owners. This is fine as long as they don't decide to have a party in the middle of the night and expect you to come and join in! Some cats learn to wake

playing with your kitten

Just like us, cats love to play. They need to do this to practice their hunting skills and also just for fun! Play is good exercise and will help to keep your kitten healthy and happy.

Games should be fun for both you and your kitten. If your cat is bored, she will probably just wander away and won't be very interested in what you are doing. If the games are too rough and your kitten uses her claws or even teeth in play, you will not enjoy it and may even get hurt. Games need to be fun *and* safe.

above *and* **below:** *This kitten shows her hunting skills with a toy bird as her "prey."*

Parental Guide !

Rough-and-tumble games, where the kitten is encouraged to bite or claw hands, feet, clothing, or hair, should never be played by any member of the family. Many cats learn that this is acceptable behavior while young, and continue it as adults. Cat bites can result in serious illness and even death, and should be prevented by insuring that human skin is treated with respect and never as prey, even in play. It is not only children who should be discouraged from playing these types of games — adults are often the worst culprits!

wand or rod toys

If your kitten is large and fast, you will need to use toys that allow you to keep away from her mouth and claws. The best ones are like fishing rods, with a long line attached that the cat can chase as you wave it around. Feathers or toys can be tied to the end of the string for the kitten to chase.

Wands are exciting and safe, because they keep you at a distance while your cat leaps and pounces to catch the toy on the end of the string. Be careful not to pull the toy away too sharply from your cat once she has caught it, as the end can get caught in her teeth and may scratch her.

above: *A full pounce! Kittens love to stalk, chase, and "kill" toys, like this clockwork mouse.*

think like a cat!

The best way to play with your kitten is to think about what kinds of games she would like to play. Most cats love stalking things that move, chasing them and catching them, either with their mouth or with their claws. You need to play games with toys, so that your cat can safely chase them and pounce on them without anyone getting hurt.

clockwork and battery-operated toys

Clockwork mice, spiders, and even frogs are available for your kitten's entertainment. These offer lots of fun and activity, but you need to watch the cat while she plays. After she has pounced on such a toy, your kitten might chew it, so you must check that any plastic or fabric parts can't be pulled off and swallowed.

New versions of these old favorites, such as a battery-driven ball which rolls and twists

around the floor, are lots of fun for large, confident kittens, but a more nervous cat might be frightened the first times the toy is used.

puzzle toys

These toys are designed to be fun and safe for your kitten to play with on her own. There are many types, usually made from strong, brightly colored plastic. They range from a ball trapped in a circular track, which the cat tries to get out with a paw, to balls that can be filled with dry cat food. Your kitten pushes the ball around to make food drop out onto the floor, so she is rewarded with food as well as amusement.

catnip toys

Catnip toys are often in the shape of furry mice, or may be balls on pieces of rope that can be picked up and carried like prey. When they smell the catnip (a type of plant) inside these toys, some cats tread their paws, dribble, and purr in pleasure. Most play with

above: *The best toys are fun for your kitten and safe for your hands.*

below: *Many cats love the smell of the catnip plant, which is contained inside some toys.*

Those that play together, stay together. Games strengthen the bond between cats and you — and between two kittens!

the toy but do not seem to enjoy the same strange but harmless effects.

homemade toys

Some of the best toys for cats are cheap and simple. Kittens love paper bags, and a bag blown up with air can keep a cat amused for hours. Place a small, lightweight ball in the bag for your kitten to pounce on, or put the bag into a safe cardboard box so that the kitten has to climb in and out to play with it.

Lengths of string and large, rolled-up balls of aluminum foil attract most kittens — even the most nervous cat will be bold enough to pounce on one of these. Be sure to supervise all "string" play to prevent any accidental string swallowing. Make sure any toys you make are large enough that your kitten can't swallow them, and never allow your cat to play with things that could hurt it, such as electric wire.

two kittens!

Rather than a toy, your kitten can play with another cat! Two kittens from the same litter often become the best of friends and happily play together for long periods. It may look frightening at first, since cats play by stalking each other, chasing, and then pouncing on one another. They also have mock battles, where they look like they are fighting, but neither cat

the thrill of the hunt

Kittens in the wild need to play to practice their hunting skills. Later on, when they are old enough to go out into the world alone, they need to hunt prey to stay alive. Hunting prey successfully takes patience, agility, and stealth. Wild cats that are not very good at hunting may go hungry!

In our homes, kittens still love to play — and not just for fun. It teaches them that humans are not prey, and increases their bond with us.

gets hurt and both are enjoying themselves.

Playing with another cat is fun and exciting for your kitten, but it shouldn't be the only type of play that they have. Kittens that grow up with a brother or sister also need to learn how to play with people too, so make time to play with each pet separately.

feeding your kitten

All cats are carnivores — they need to eat meat to survive. One look at their sharp teeth shows us that they are designed to hunt prey and kill it.

In our homes, we do not expect our pet cats to find their own dinner. Instead, we buy them food that will keep them healthy and happy. There are many different types of cat food; what is best to give your kitten depends on the size and age of your pet and the cost of the food. You will probably also find that your cat prefers certain types and brands of food.

above: *All mine! A kitten pulls the remains of some food closer to himself.*

where to feed

Cats like to eat in places where they feel safe. It is best to choose one area, so your kitten knows where he will be fed every time. Most cats like to eat on a raised surface, off the floor, then they can see around them while they eat and feel safer — they are unlikely to be ambushed by another pet or accidentally stepped on! The area that you choose should be quiet and well away from the litter box.

Most cats prefer to be fed on a high surface, where they feel safe.

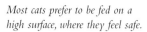

above: *Cats enjoy meal-time companionship....*

below: *...But make sure each gets his own share.*

how much food?

Most cats like to eat small meals several times every day, to keep up their energy, rather than have one or two big meals. If you give your kitten dry food, he will probably return to his food many times during the day and night to eat as much as he needs. If you give canned food or fresh meat, you need to offer small amounts several times a day. A kitten of eight to 12 weeks old will probably need five small meals a day to allow his digestive system to work properly.

no vegetarian cats

Cats cannot be vegetarian. This is because they need very specific nutrients found only in meat, including vitamin A and niacin, and they cannot produce taurine within their body, which is vital for their eyes to work properly.

kinds of food

Kittens need special food designed to give them all the good nutrition they need to grow and have lots of energy. The choice of canned and dry foods is huge, and the ones you give your pet may depend on what your family can afford.

Dry foods smell less than meat and can be left out all day without attracting flies or other insects. They also help to keep your cat's teeth clean, as the kitten needs to crunch it up to eat it. Canned foods are more tasty and may appeal to your kitten more. However, they cannot be left out all day and some may upset your kitten's stomach.

If you wish to change your kitten's diet

from dry to canned food, from canned to dry, or introduce a type of food he hasn't had before, always do so very gradually. Changing the type of food too quickly can cause stomach upsets and diarrhea and make a young kitten seriously ill.

Your veterinarian can give advice if you are not sure what to feed your kitten.

water

Your kitten should always be able to reach his own bowl of fresh, clean drinking water. If he eats canned food he may hardly drink at all, as he will get water from the food. If your kitten eats dry food, he will need to drink more often, so make extra sure that he always has fresh water.

If your kitten suddenly starts drinking more water than usual, he may be ill. Tell an adult and ask your veterinarian if you are worried.

above: *Kittens soon learn to expect food from their owners. Give treats to reward your cat's good behavior.*

It might surprise you to learn that you should not give milk to cats! Once weaned, a kitten does not need milk in his diet and cow's milk can upset his stomach. If you want to give your cat a treat, milk specially made for cats is available in many stores.

treats

There are almost as many food treats to buy as there are dry and canned foods. Treats are used to reward your cat for being smart, or given once in a while just because you love him!

pica

Some cats have the strange habit of chewing and eating wool, plastic, rubber, and even electrical cables. "Pica" is the name for this habit of eating things that aren't food. Siamese and Burmese cats are most likely to do this, although others also chew things. If your cat starts this odd behavior, seek help from your veterinarian immediately, as it can be very dangerous.

left: *It is natural for cats to eat grass. Do not worry if he vomits afterward.*

Treats come in all shapes and flavors, from fish treats to chocolate drops. If you do not want to buy specially made treats, you can give tiny pieces of cooked chicken or fish instead, but make sure they do not have any bones in them, as these can get stuck in your kitten's throat or make him seriously ill.

The chocolate that we eat is highly poisonous to animals and should never be given. If you can't find chocolate drops specially designed for cats, give another food treat instead.

It is important that you do not allow your cat to have other human food, by allowing him to steal from your plate or feeding him bits from your plate while you are eating. Your cat will become a real nuisance if he learns he can get food from the dinner table.

eating grass

Nearly all cats chew on fresh grass if they get the chance. This is normal and is thought to help their digestion. Occasionally, your kitten might vomit after eating grass, but as long as he is otherwise healthy, this is nothing to worry about.

If your kitten is kept indoors, you may want to give him fresh grass to chew on. Pet stores sell small containers of planted seeds that can be grown on your windowsill so that your cat can nibble at it whenever he wants.

Grass is thought to aid cats' digestion, so if you keep your kitten indoors, you may want to grow some for him.

how kittens learn

In the first few weeks and months of life, your kitten has a lot to learn. She is like a sponge, ready to soak up all the information she can and learn from her experiences.

Kittens don't go to school, so how do they learn? Just like us, cats form habits depending on what they enjoy and what they don't like. If they find that something is fun and rewarding, they are likely to do it again. If they don't get a reward for something they did, or something unpleasant happened when they did it, they probably won't do it again.

So if you give your kitten a reward — food, toys, or your attention — for coming to you when you call

Cats learn by trial and success, so if something they do earns a reward, they are likely to do it again.

her, she will probably want to do it again. If you call her but then give her nothing or ignore her, she will think twice before coming to you next time.

Unfortunately, this also means that your kitten can easily learn to do things that you don't want her to do. For example, your

kitten might try to climb the drapes. Everyone turns and watches her, and laughs. Your kitten would enjoy the attention and carry on with what she's doing and certainly do it again — because it was fun. This might be okay with a small kitten, but if she grew up with this habit, her claws would make

left: *Many cats find it fun and rewarding to play with and even climb the drapes.*

holes in the drapes and your family would be angry. Then she might be shouted at for doing something that she was once rewarded for — very difficult for a cat to understand.

Try to make sure that you only reward your kitten for behavior that you like and that will be suitable when she's an adult. Ignore behavior that your don't like, or deal with it calmly if you can't ignore it. Your cat can find it fun to annoy you!

cat burglar

Cats are very curious creatures. As they are so agile, it is easy for them to explore every nook and cranny, and this includes jumping onto tables and kitchen surfaces. If your kitten jumps onto a table and finds some delicious food left there, she will think she has won the kitty lottery! It is very likely that she will make a habit of jumping onto the table to see if there is something to eat there.

If the cat is going to be left

alone, even for a few minutes, always make sure that you put food out of reach or shut in a cupboard. Some cats try almost any kind of food, while others are quite choosy, but don't leave it to chance. The best way to keep your kitten off the counter tops and tables is to make sure that there's no reason to get up there in the first place!

warm and snug

Cats love to rest somewhere cozy and warm. Their favorite places are often those areas where the smell of their owners is strongest, too. Most cats choose to rest on couches or beds where their owners also like to sit or sleep.

Uh-oh! This laundry hamper has become a kitty playground.

Cats always find the best places to sleep — usually in your chair!

If you don't want your cat to get on your bed or sit on your favorite chair, prevention is better than cure. Shut your bedroom door so your cat can't go in there, or put a cushion, bag, or a sheet of aluminum foil on your chair seat if you want to stop her putting her dirty paws on it. There is no point scolding your cat if she is already in a place where you don't want her to be. If you don't block the area, she will wait until you are out of sight before going back there!

boredom

Some cats get into trouble simply because they are bored at home by themselves. This is particularly true of cats kept indoors, who may not have enough to do to keep them busy.

If your cat claws or chews things around the home, or behaves in a naughty way, try to think why she is doing it. Does she get attention from it? Could she be bored or lonely? Is she trying to demand food or attention? Seeing the problem from your cat's point of view may help you solve the problem.

Clearly uncomfortable with the way she is being held, this kitten makes a jump for freedom.

punishment

It is never a good idea to punish your cat, no matter how naughty she has been. Cats do not understand our language or our rules. Although they eventually learn what a few words mean, like "dinner" and "sit," they can never understand what we say to them or the way we act.

For example, we might like it when our cat cuddles up next to us in bed one night, but be annoyed when she walks across the bedclothes with muddy paws the next day. Your cat will not understand that having dirty feet made you angry, only that you were suddenly in a bad mood for no reason!

Try to be consistent with your kitten in the home. Make a list of rules that everyone in the family agrees to. For example, will your cat be fed at certain times, or at any time when she asks? Will she be allowed to get on beds or furniture?

The set of rules will be different for every family, but there will be less arguments when they are set out in advance, as everyone will know what the kitten is allowed to do and what she isn't.

Don't put temptation in your kitten's way. She won't be able to resist tasty food, so don't leave any where she can get to it.

petting and biting

Cats are peaceful animals. They prefer to run away than be aggressive, but sometimes they show defensive behavior if they are frightened or feel cornered. Some cats do this when they are being petted. One minute, they are sitting on your lap, enjoying being stroked, and the next they are spitting and hissing and look angry. This probably happens when the cat feels overwhelmed and a little trapped by your attention.

If your cat does this, next time pet her while she sits on the couch next to you, rather then on your lap, and only stroke her for a short period of time. If she doesn't move away, stroke her again for a little while, then stop. This gives her the chance to move away if she wants to.

training your kitten
1 using a cat flap

You may have chosen to keep your cat indoors all the time, but if he is going to be allowed to go outside, it is useful to fit a cat flap. This is a small door that is set into the back door of your house and allows your kitten to come and go whenever he wants. The door closes behind him automatically, but he can get back in again simply by pushing it with his paws or nose.

Most cats love the freedom of being able to go outside whenever they want, but your kitten will have to learn how to open the door for himself. Never push your kitten through the opening and never push his paws or head against the door to show him what to do. You could make him scared of cat flaps.

step by step

1. Hold the flap open, using a lump of modeling clay or a piece of rolled-up adhesive tape wedged in the hinge, or prop it open with a stick. Your kitten will be able to see outdoors through the hole.

2. Take the kitten outside, so he will be moving toward the home that he is used to. Ask an adult to gently hold your kitten outside the door; inside, call the kitten's name and hold a food treat or favorite toy where he can see it, to encourage him to come through the hole.

3. As soon as he comes through the hole, give your kitten the food treat or toy. Repeat steps 1 to 3 several times, until the kitten is happy to come through the hole into the home.

4. Next switch over, so someone has the kitten inside the house while you call him through to the outside world. Use food treats and repeat the steps until your kitten is completely confident walking in and out through the hole.

5. Now it's time to lower the flap, so the kitten has to push it to get through the hole. Start by wedging or propping the flap halfway open. Encourage the kitten to push against the barrier to reach you and his reward on the other side. Do this several times in both directions, so the kitten knows he must push the flap, whether he's going outside or coming back inside.

6. Lower the flap a little more and let your kitten practice again. Soon your kitten will learn to push the flap the whole way. Don't force your kitten — if he can use the flap at one level but not when it is a little lower, raise the flap again and keep practicing before moving on again.

no exit

Many cat owners let their pets outside during the day but keep them inside at night, to keep them safe from road traffic. If your family does this, your kitten needs to understand that he cannot go through the flap when it is locked. Although we can see that the flap is locked in place, a cat may not understand why he cannot push the flap open, when he could earlier in the day.

Putting a "signal" next to or across the flap is useful. The cat learns to associate the signal with the flap being shut, so he doesn't try to break out! The signal can be a towel hung up next to the flap or a piece of board placed across it. Your kitten will soon learn that the signal means "no exit."

Remember to remove the signal when the flap is open again or the system won't work.

above: *Propping the flap wide open will help your kitten work out how to use the door.*

opposite page *and* **below:** *Encourage your kitten to come through the door, first going into the house, then the opposite direction, toward the yard.*

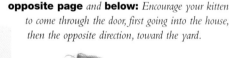

2 using a scratching post

All cats need to scratch things to keeps their claws in good condition. Cats also leave scent behind when they scratch, to leave messages for other cats (*see page 33*). Given the opportunity, most cats prefer to scratch on tree trunks or upright posts outdoors. However, if your kitten cannot go outside yet, or if you are keeping him indoors, you will need to provide a scratching post or pad for him in your home.

There are lots of scratching posts you can buy, or you could use a section of a large tree branch. Cats like to reach up and stretch while they scratch, so the post needs to be at least as tall as your kitten when he is standing on his hind legs. You can buy a big post when you get your kitten, to allow for your pet's size when he is older, or get a new scratching post when he is fully grown.

using the post

Position the post or pad in a quiet place, so your kitten feels safe

The scratching posts built into this activity center are keeping the kittens' claws sharp and saving the furniture from damage!

when he uses the post. Encourage him to use the scratching post, rather than the end of your couch, by making the post as attractive as possible.

First, make sure that the post smells like your home and is familiar to your kitten. Most cats are suspicious of new objects

and will sniff them to see if they recognize their smell. Simply leave the scratching post where it can be seen, then your kitten will gradually get used to the smell and sight of it.

You can also trick your kitten into thinking the post has been there for a long time. Encourage your kitten to rub your hands with his face and cheeks. Most cats do this just to show that they are friendly.

If yours doesn't, don't force him to do it, but stroke him and talk to him quietly. This puts a little of his smell onto your hands.

sharp operator

Cats are one of the very few animals that can extend and retract their claws whenever they want to. They extend them for hunting and climbing, so the claws stick out and make it easier to hold things, then retract them back inside the foot when they don't need them. It would be tricky for a cat to walk if its claws were always extended! Dogs and even one of the cat's larger relatives, the cheetah, cannot extend and retract their claws.

Immediately rub your hands over the post to put some of his smell and your smell onto it, then it will seem familiar to the kitten.

If your kitten still doesn't pay any attention to the post and scratches somewhere else, encourage him to use the post by attaching some string or a toy from the top. He will play on or around it and put his paws on the scratching post almost by accident. You can then praise him and play with him as a reward for using the post.

scratching pads

Some cats prefer scratching along the ground, instead of using a vertical post. If your kitten scratches the floor, protect the carpet by using a scratching pad laid flat on the ground. Follow the same "using the post" instructions.

Cats need to stretch up to scratch properly, so make sure the post is tall enough.

3 coming when called

One of easiest and most useful commands to train your kitten is to come to you when he is called. No matter where your kitten is, you can find him by calling to make him come running to you.

Most kittens naturally learn to come when called — except they wait to hear the sound of their food being prepared! This is how you train your cat to come to you — using food as a reward.

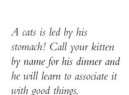

Encourage your kitten to come to you by luring him with a food treat.

A cats is led by his stomach! Call your kitten by name for his dinner and he will learn to associate it with good things.

step by step

1. Every time you feed your kitten, call him to you first. Most kittens are given several small meals each day, so these times are ideal for this training.

2. First call your kitten even if he is right in front of you when you are going to feed him. Use his name, and the same word each time. For example, "Tiger, come!" — then immediately give him food that he really likes. If he ignores you, lure him toward you with a food treat or toy. If he still ignores you, try again later when he is more hungry or more alert.

3. Over the next few days, call your kitten before you get his food out. This will mean that he answers to the sound of your voice, rather than the sound of the food package being opened.

4. Gradually increase the distance between you and your kitten before calling him. You may need someone else to help you. Ask them to play a game with him in one room, then you can call him to you

in another room before you feed him. If he ignores you, don't be angry or chase after him, just don't give him the food.

5. Give different rewards when your kitten comes to your call. It won't always be dinner time, so at different times give lots of praise and stroking, a really tasty food treat, or an exciting game with a toy. It is the reward that will insure your cat will continue to come when you call, so be generous!

6. Never call your kitten to you for something unpleasant, even if you don't mean it to be. This includes spraying with

Cats are intelligent but need gentle motivation to respond to their name being called.

be kind

Cats can be trained to do all kinds of tasks, just like dogs, but they always need to be trained with gentleness and kindness. Being angry with a cat for doing something wrong will mean that he is even less likely to want to be with you. Never shout at your kitten or smack him if he doesn't understand what you want him to do. Start the training again and teach him slowly and carefully.

flea spray, nail clipping, and bathing. Your kitten will associate the negative experience with coming when called and will choose to stay away.

Be patient when you train your kitten. If he is anxious or distracted, try again later.

4 sitting and begging on command

sitting on command

Cats can be trained to sit when asked, just like dogs. This is useful if you want to keep your kitten in one place for a short time — to take a photograph of him, for example. It also looks very impressive to your friends and family!

Teaching your kitten to sit is easy if he knows you will give him a reward for it. Use really tasty treats, such as cooked chicken or fish, and be patient.

above: *Even young kittens can be trained to sit.*

left: *Use a food treat to lure the kitten into position.*

1. Standing in front of him, show your kitten that you have a food treat.
2. Hold the food above his head so he has to look right up at you.
3. As he lifts his head high, his bottom will go down toward the floor and he will sit. Immediately say "good," and then give him the treat. If your kitten jumps up to get to your hand, lower the treat a little and ignore him until he is sitting.
4. Practice at different times and places until your kitten sits when you lift your hand. Now you can use the word "sit" just before he sits.
5. Eventually, you may be able to get your kitten to sit just by using the command word, without the food treat or hand movement.

above: *Training should be fun for both of you. Keep a diary of your kitten's progress.*

left: *This kitten is excellent at "being a bear"! It takes lots of practice to train a cat to sit up and beg this high into the air.*

begging on command

You can teach your kitten to sit up and beg, just like a dog! This trick is also called "be a meer-cat," because this is how these prairie animals look when they are scanning the horizon, or "be a bear."

1. Find a food treat that your kitten really likes, such as tiny pieces of chicken or a cat treat from the pet store.
2. Hold the treat just above your kitten's nose and lure him into a sitting position, as you did when teaching him to sit.
3. Lift your hand a tiny bit so that your kitten's front feet come off the ground a little. As soon as they do, say "good" and give him the treat.

4. Repeat this until your kitten lifts his front feet a little higher. If he jumps up at your hand, say nothing, wait, and start again at step 2.
5. Practice until your kitten lifts his paws so high that he's sitting almost upright and begs when you move your hand above his head. You will probably find that he will do this trick whenever he wants something!

film stars

Cats have been trained to perform in films. Some can do amazing tricks, like open doors and ring bells on command. Just think what you can teach your cat to do, with time and patience!

5 retrieving objects

Cats can be taught to bring toys back to you — some thoroughly enjoy a game of "fetch"! Cats carry prey in their mouths, and mother cats carry their kittens from place to place, so it's natural for them to retrieve things.

You need to be patient when you are trying to teach a kitten to retrieve. Some learn it quickly, particularly Oriental cat breeds, such as the Siamese and Burmese; others take longer to teach.

Playing "fetch" with your kitten is a good way to give him exercise and to keep him from becoming bored. Many cats will learn to run out after a small toy or something similar and carry it back to their owner, just like a dog! Playing games of all kinds is especially important for cats that are kept indoors, to keep them happy and active.

above: *Nearly all cats will hold toys during play, so keep the training fun and your kitten will retrieve.*

It's not only dogs that can learn to retrieve — cats will run after and pick up toys, too.

It's natural for cats to chase and grab things. This instinct can be used to retrieve toys.

step by step

1. First teach your kitten to come to you when you call him. This is explained on pages 68–69.

2. Get a small, light toy that your kitten really enjoys playing with. A soft toy mouse or short length of sisal rope are ideal. Play a game with the toy, pulling or rolling it along the floor while the kitten chases and grabs it. The more the toy is like prey, dashing around like a real mouse, the more your kitten will be interested in it. Move it around at different speeds and in different directions, and hide it behind pieces of furniture.

3. When your kitten is really excited by this chasing game, let go of the toy and allow him to pick it up.

4. As soon as your kitten has got the toy, call him to you. When he is close to you, offer him another toy or food treat in place of the prey toy that he caught.

5. Do not have a tug-of-war for the toy. If he runs off with it, encourage him back to you and play another game; do not try to take the toy out of his mouth or from between his claws.

6. Keep practicing. It will probably take many attempts to teach your kitten how to pick up toys and carry them to you. If he is reluctant to play, try a different game or trick, or try again later — he may be feeling tired, hungry, or just quiet.

use your imagination!

There are many tricks that you can teach your kitten — see how many you can invent and work out how best to encourage the cat to perform them. Here are some suggestions:

- Give a paw
- Roll over
- Jump up onto a chair and sit
- Jump from one stool or chair to another
- Run through a homemade tunnel (an empty cardboard box on its side)

understanding
kitten communication
1 body language

Cats can't speak to us; they have a language all of their own. Kittens learn how to use body language from their mother and litter-mates, working out how to tell each other things with movements of their tail, eyes, and ears and understanding what the body signals of other cats mean, too.

eyes

A cat's eyes reveal a lot about how she is feeling. Cats can narrow their eyes into thin slits or open them wide in a stare.

A cat that is relaxed and content half-closes her eyes. She blinks very slowly and turns her face away from whoever is watching her.

Cats that are scared usually have wide eyes and dilated pupils — the black center part of the eye becomes wide and round.

Angry cats may also have their eyes wide open, but the pupils narrow to thin slits.

ears

Cats' ears may be small, but they are highly mobile! Thirty different muscles move the ears, and allow them to turn left and right, as well as back and up. Cats' ears can move independently of one another, so one can turn to listen in one direction while the other goes the opposite way!

Relaxed cats usually hold their ears facing forward and tilted back at a slight angle. If something interests the cat, the ears prick up

above: *The cat's ears are raised, flattened, and turned using 30 muscles.*

left: *Narrowing the eyes is a friendly signal.*

The tail held straight up is a friendly greeting.

straight up in the air, perhaps with the tip bent over at an angle.

A relaxed and contented cat simply lets its tail hang down.

A cat that is angry, or is thinking about pouncing on something, may gently swish its tail from side to side. A tail thrashing from side to side is definitely a warning, as the cat is either very excited or aggressive. You are most likely to see this if your cat is watching birds outside the window and is frustrated that she can't reach them!

Kittens sometimes show a "play tail." The tail forms an upside down U shape and means the kitten is being playful. It is sometimes seen when the kitten dashes around the house in a strange sideways gambol (*see page 28*).

A cat that is feeling angry or very frightened might fluff up her tail until all the hair stands on end. With her tail held upright, it will be as big and noticeable as possible, to try frightening off another cat or a dog that she feels is threatening. When the tail becomes this wide and fluffy it is known as a "bottle brush" tail.

slightly, to catch the sound.

Cats that are frightened flatten their ears so that they lie right against their heads. This is a clear warning to move away.

Angry cats also give clues about how they are feeling by turning their ears around so that the backs of the ears are shown and the insides of the earflaps face to the sides.

tail

Cats use their tails to tell us how they feel. You will soon know if a kitten is happy to see you — she will run toward you with her tail held

If a cat is fearful of another animal, she will arch her back and fluff her tail.

2 scent messages

To us, smells can be nice or nasty, but to cats they are vitally important. Cats have a very sensitive sense of smell and use scent to communicate with each other.

Cats recognize each other by the way they smell. They don't even have to see each other to know who's been in their neighborhood, at what time, and for how long! All this information can be gained by sniffing where another cat has been.

In the home, with us, cats are also aware of scent. They recognize the people in their family more by how they smell than how they look, because after a cat has been living somewhere for a short while, her scent has spread around so every person smells familiar — they have the "clan odor."

When a cat rubs her cheeks against

Cats rub themselves against furniture so it smells familiar and they feel secure.

someone, a trace of her scent is left behind. We cannot see or smell it, but it this scent that makes your kitten feel comfortable with you. You will see your kitten rubbing her chin and face on your furniture, too. She does this so objects, as well as people, smell as she does, letting her feel safe in the home.

This comforting and familiar scent fades away, so to keep it around her your kitten will rub things every day. Most cats have favorite spots where they do this — the edge of a couch, for example, or the bottom step of the stairs. Scent marking is completely harmless to us and our furniture, so you can encourage your cat to rub as much as she likes!

Cats have other ways of spreading their

Cats live in a world of scents, indoors and out.

personal cat smell

All cats have their own individual smell. This is so unique that it acts like a feline fingerprint and is recognized by other cats who know them. Some medicines accidentally change this personal smell for a while, so two cats might not recognize each other if one has been to the veterinarian. To avoid this problem, keep one cat in a room with you for a while before reintroducing her to your other cat.

scent around. Outdoors, they scratch things, which releases scent from between their foot pads onto trees and fences, and use urine marking and even their feces to tell other cats that they have been in the area. Unfortunately, a cat that is feeling anxious or stressed might mark their indoor territory like this. If your kitten messes in the home because of stress, ask your veterinarian for advice.

above: *This kitten is rubbing herself against the girl in a friendly greeting.*

spreading the scent

If you are introducing something new into the home, such as a piece of furniture or even a person, you can make sure that your kitten is not frightened by it. Using a piece of clean cloth, such as a handkerchief or a wash cloth, encourage your kitten to rub on the cloth while you hold it. Rub the cloth on the new item or person, at cat chin height, before the kitten first meets them. Your kitten will think that the new object or person is familiar, as she will seem to have rubbed on them already.

Cats sniff where other cats have been to gain information about them.

3 purring and meowing

Cats also use sounds to communicate with each other and with us — what could be more cat-like than a "meow"? Some breeds of cat are very talkative. They like to chatter to their owner all the time, and may even "shout" if they are ignored! Siamese cats are one of the noisiest.

Mother cats spend a great deal of time communicating with their kittens. A mother calls to them when she comes home and purrs when the kittens are feeding. Kittens call to their mother when they are worried, and it is thought that each kitten sounds different, so the mother can easily find each one.

above: *Cats purr to show that they feel comfortable, secure, and happy.*

purring

Cats make a purring sound when they are happy. Even kittens can do this, and they often purr when they are feeding from their mother.

Cats keep their mouths closed when they purr. They don't need to stop purring to take breaths so they can do it for a long time.

mysterious sound

No one knows how cats purr. It is thought that they vibrate their vocal cords in a special way, but whether this is true remains a mystery.

meowing

Most "talking" sounds are made by the cat opening her mouth and then closing it at the end of the sound. Your cat may meow, mew,

Kittens purr to communicate with their mother in the nest, telling her they are content. They can keep purring while feeding from their mother.

Most cats use several different meows to communicate with their owner. This kitten wants to be rescued!

chirrup, or even sound a little like she is singing!

Most cats notice that humans respond to these sounds and eventually we can learn what some of the "words" mean. Each cat's words are a little different from another's, but you will soon find out what sounds your

kitten uses to ask to come in, go out, be given food, be petted, and when she is annoyed with you.

Some owners have identified over 16 different sounds that their cat makes — and each can have a different meaning. Can you work out what your cat is saying to you?

hissing and growling

Cats hiss when they are frightened and when they are trying to scare another cat or a dog away. Cats can also growl. This sound, made deep in the back of the cat's throat, is a clear warning to keep away.

yowling

This long, musical sound is made by the cat opening her mouth then closing it slightly to alter the tone of her voice. Yowling is usually designed to get attention, and if owners aren't careful, can become an annoying habit. A song may be nice to hear during the day, but doesn't sound so good in the middle of the night when you are trying to sleep!

rare roar

Our pet cats cannot roar like their lion cousins. This is because a special area at the back of a lion's throat is different from your kitten's.

left: *Hisses and growls are used to try to make people or animals go away.*

talking to your kitten

Humans talk to each other by using speech. We shout, laugh, whisper, cry, and chat to tell each other how we feel. Cats use body language instead, and are mostly silent when they communicate with each other. The only times cats really talk to each other using sound are when they purr to show happiness, when they are angry with each other, and when looking for a mate. Female cats make a loud wailing noise when they are trying to attract a male cat. This sound is known as "calling."

Once you understand what your kitten is trying to say to you with his body language, it is easier to make your feelings known to him. Many owners get so good at communicating with their cat that they can have a kind of conversation, each taking it in turns to "talk" and then waiting for the other to reply. This is done without words, since kittens do not understand our language, aside from special words, like their name and "dinner"! To talk to your kitten, act like a cat and let your face and body do the talking!

Have a "conversation" with your kitten by copying his movements and facial expressions.

how to talk to your kitten

1. Choose a time when you and your kitten are sitting together quietly.
2. Watch your kitten closely. If he looks at you, see if he then narrows his eyes and turns his face away slightly.
3. As soon as he does this, copy him by half-closing your own eyes and turning your face away.
4. Your kitten is likely to respond by looking back at you, then looking away again.

Cats learn to recognize members of their family by their scent — rubbing on people makes them smell familiar.

5. Continue to "reply" to your kitten. Try to breathe at the same speed he does, and match his facial expression and movements, keeping quiet and very still.

talking cat and dogs

Cats don't only communicate with each other and with us, they can also be great friends with other animals, such as dogs. If you own a dog, it is important that he should never be allowed to chase your cat, or the cat will be scared of him. Cats and dogs can learn to live together and enjoy each other's company. Some cats rub their canine friends, so that they share the clan odor, and many greet each other if they have been apart. Many cats and dogs share the same bed, snuggle up together for warmth, and even eat together.

perfume power

In addition to talking to your cat with body language, it is important to smell just right! The family smell that the cat spreads by rubbing things — the "clan odor" — helps him to recognize us and form close bonds with us. Encouraging your kitten to rub on you helps this system, since we wash our hands and use deodorants and other strong-smelling preparations that disguise our usual smell.

To encourage your kitten to rub his face and chin on your hands, first wait for him to come to you. It is bad cat manners to walk up to your kitten and force attention on him, so sit quietly and allow your hand to hang down. Wait for your kitten to approach, and see if he rubs your hand. If he does, gently stroke behind his ears and around his face. This will help to spread his scent.

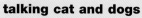

Use food to strengthen your relationship with your cat — friends like to go to dinner together!

Some timid cats prefer to rub around your legs, and most cats do this when they are hungry and see that you have their food! If this is the only time that your cat rubs on you, take a while to put the food into the dish, to make the most of this scent rubbing.

accidental friends

You may notice that people who don't like cats very much find that themselves being pestered by your kitten when they come to visit! This because when we don't like something, we tend to turn our heads away and pull a face that narrows our eyes — which is like an invitation to the cat to come for attention!

Body language shows that these two kittens are fearful of each other. They may even show aggression to try to scare away the other cat.

becoming friends

Unlike dogs, cats are not social animals. In the wild, they are not designed to live in close contact with other cats and don't think of other cats as part of the family. However, in our homes, many cats seem to form friendships with one another, particularly litter-mates, who are used to being together from birth. Cats that get along well together spend a lot of time grooming each other, licking each other, and resting closely together, so that they share the same scent. This means that each cat thinks of the other as part of its family.

above: *Kittens using scent and facial expressions to greet each other.*

below: *Use food and gently stroking to calm a shy kitten.*

greeting a shy kitten

If your kitten is shy, do not try to force him to make friends with you. Instead, sit in the same room and ignore him. If he comes near you, turn your face away from him, sit very quietly, and narrow your eyes. Out of the corner of your eye you should see that he will start to trust you and begin to come closer. Feed him somewhere nearby to make your kitten feel even more secure.

mealtime friends

If your kitten is very nervous and shy, you can make friends by stroking and petting him while he is eating. He will start to associate you and your touch with good things. Make sure that the food is really tasty, and feed your cat on a high surface so that he does not feel vulnerable. Stroke him from head to tail, firmly but gently two or three times while he is eating, but allow him to jump down and have time to himself whenever he wants.

fun things to do with your kitten

1 games to play indoors

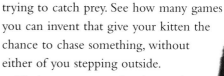

All cats have to spend some time indoors. This may be because the weather is bad or because it is not safe to allow them outside. Whatever the reason, your kitten will be happy in the home if you keep him busy. If the cat is kept indoors all the time, it is even more important that you play games with him so he isn't bored.

chase games

Outdoors, cats love to chase anything that moves things, such as insects or leaves blowing in the wind — it's like they are

trying to catch prey. See how many games you can invent that give your kitten the chance to chase something, without either of you stepping outside.

All chase games need to have rules. The most important one is that the

Kittens will play in, on, and with just about anything!

play safe

It is very important that you always play carefully and safely, so there is no chance that you, your kitten, or anyone else will get hurt. Whether you are playing inside or outside, follow these rules:

● Do not use anything as a cat toy that can easily break and hurt you or the kitten

● Do not push anything against the cat's body or pull him along

● Only play with things that belong to you or the kitten — the owner will be very angry if you damage something valuable!

● Do not play with or near water, especially deep water like a pond or full bathtub

● Cats can easily be scared by loud noises, so keep your kitten indoors or shut in another room if you are having a party — balloons bursting or fireworks going off can be terrifying for your cat

kitten is not allowed to chase you, your hands, or your feet. Cats have sharp claws and fast reactions, and as they grow they become more and more powerful. If an adult cat grabs a person with their claws, it can really hurt.

how to make a wand toy

1. Get a short stick, or length of bamboo cane, about 12 inches (25cm) long. If it's too long, ask an adult to shorten it for you.
2. Wrap the ends of the stick with lots of plastic tape so they are not sharp.
3. Tie a long piece of string onto one end of the stick, so it looks like a fishing line.
4. Tie exciting things to chase on the other end of the string — feathers, a few strands of yarn or cat toys, for example. Now you have a play wand, dangle it in front of your kitten and make it exciting for him to chase.

Wand toys

Wand toys are ideal for safe chasing games. Many pet stores sell wonderful wand toys, or you can make one yourself.

Hold the wand like a fishing rod, then pull the string quickly along the floor and up into the air for your cat to chase. Do not to tug the string if your kitten grabs hold of the end, let the string go limp instead. When your kitten lets go, encourage him to chase again.

Once your kitten is used to this game, you can make it more difficult. Drag the end of the

Wand toys are ideal because they are lots of fun for you and your kitten and keep your hands safely away from sharp claws and teeth.

string slowly away from the kitten around the back of the couch or past an open door. Watch how your cat crouches to stalk the string and then try to pounce on it. See if you can pull it out of the way before the kitten grabs it — you'll soon find out who's fastest!

Roll the ball

Many kittens enjoy chasing a cat ball. These are usually hollow and light, and may have a bell or some catnip inside to make them even more exciting. Your kitten will love to chase the ball if you roll it along the floor for him.

Balls always end up underneath the furniture, so when you are bored of fetching it, put the ball inside a large cardboard box with an open top. Your kitten can get into the box and chase the ball around to his heart's content, without it disappearing under the couch!

Make sure any balls are too big for your cat to accidentally swallow.

Bags of fun

A very cheap toy that kittens find lots of fun is a paper bag (never a plastic one). You can make it more exciting by scrunching up the neck of the bag and blowing into it, a little like a balloon, so your kitten can leap onto it.

Put a cat ball or a few dry food treats inside the bag and watch your kitten try to get them out again.

searching games

Cats like to search for things, just like they search for prey before chasing it. Cats use their eyes, ears, and sense of smell when they are out hunting, so searching games use all of their natural skills.

Find the treat

This game is very simple. Find a food treat that your kitten really enjoys, such as a small piece of cooked chicken or some treats bought at a pet store. Hide the treat in one room while your kitten is in another, then encourage him to find it.

Make this game easy to begin with, so that

make a play loop

1. Gather several safe objects, such as a feather, a catnip mouse, and an old table tennis ball or other hollow plastic ball.

2. Ask an adult to help you attach the toys onto a long piece of cord, using cotton thread to tie things to the cord and by making two holes in the ball so the cord can pass through. Tie the ends of the cord together, to make a loop.

3. Hang the looped cord over a door handle or over the top of the stair rail at the bottom banister of your stairs. Your kitten will have a great time discovering that whenever he jumps up at something on the cord, the loop is pulled around and another toy appears!

your kitten gets the idea. When he is good at it, try placing the treat inside a cardboard tube and see whether your kitten can find it and then hook the treat out with a paw.

Food scattering

If you are feeding your kitten dry food, there is no reason why your cat should not hunt for it. Rather than giving all the food in a dish, throw a few nuggets of dry food so your kitten has to hunt for them. Don't scatter the pieces far from the bowl or use too many to begin with; make it easy enough that your kitten enjoys the game. When he has learned that he has to find some of his food, you can drop it over a wider area, but ask an adult before you start spreading cat food throughout the home!

activity centers

If your kitten is going to live indoors all the time, it is important that he can do all the things that an outdoor cat can — he needs space to run, jump, climb, and "hunt." A cat activity center, made of platforms, posts, and dangling toys for your kitten to play with, are perfect for this purpose. The kitten can climb up to different levels to explore, or find a high place to sleep or watch everything that's happening in the room. Ready-made "cat gyms" are expensive, so you ask an adult

to help you make one of your own.

Planning your activity center is the most important part. Think about what cats like to do. A rope hanging from the ceiling will allow him to climb. Shelves set all the way up the wall can be a kitten staircase, while cardboard boxes can be stacked on the floor to make a maze that your kitten has to run through to find a reward. Ask an adult to help you with your activity center, and always use things that are safe for your cat to play on.

above: *Hide and seek! A cardboard box can provide hours of fun.*

left: *Set up an activity center and train your kitten to jump.*

2 going outdoors

Kittens must have all of their vaccinations before they are allowed outside. Booster vaccinations, given as often as every three months or long as a year apart, help to keep cats healthy. The type and timing of vaccinations required depend on where you live, but your veterinarian will set a vaccination program for your kitten.

Even if your kitten has completed his vaccinations when you bring him home, he needs to be kept indoors for three to four weeks before being allowed outdoors. This is to allow him to become happy with your home, so he wants to return after he is let out.

Cats are designed to hunt and play in the open air, but going outside for the first time must seem strange.

You may be a little anxious the first time that you let your kitten outside, but cats have a very good "homing instinct." You will notice that after your kitten leaves the house, he will keep looking back so he knows how to get home.

dangers outdoors

Outside, your kitten will need to beware of dangers. The worst is road traffic. If you live near a busy road, allowing your kitten outside

going outside for the first time

1. Let your kitten out early in the day. This gives him time to look around outside and still be able to get home long before it starts to get dark.

2. Before you let the kitten outside, ask an adult to cook some delicious food that has a strong smell — fish is ideal. Do not give your kitten any of the food: it is a reward to give him when he comes back.

3. When you let your kitten outside, open the door and allow him to walk out for himself — do not carry him. This is for two reasons: Your kitten may just want to sit and look at first, and go further when he is ready. The other reason is that cats have scent glands between their foot pads, so as he walks out of the door, your kitten will leave a scent trail that he can follow home again.

4. If your kitten is confident and walks outside, go with him and encourage him to explore by talking to him. See if he will play with a toy. If not, just let the kitten look around.

5. After a few minutes, encourage your kitten to follow you back into the house, and then immediately give him some of the food that was cooked earlier.

6. Repeat this every day, gradually increasing the time he has outdoors before calling him in for food. Eventually your kitten will be happy outside, even on his own, and come home by himself, then you can let him come and go when he wants by opening the cat flap (*see pages 64–65*).

on his own may be too dangerous. You can walk him on a harness and leash or have tall fences set around the yard — cats are excellent climbers and can easily scale an eight-foot fence!

Cats are outdoor creatures — they love lying in the sun, chasing leaves, and running and jumping in freedom. As most accidents happen at night, keeping your kitten indoors during the night and allowing him out during the day is the best idea.

It will probably take some time before your cat is really confident about going outside. At first, some kittens are nervous about going to the toilet outdoors, because it leaves a message for other cats that there's a new cat in the neighborhood. If there is a litter box in your home, he can simply go indoors when he needs the toilet.

The great outdoors offers many new experiences and some surprises. This kitten is spitting out the seeds of a plant he has been eating.

Plants

Cats instinctively eat grass from time to time; this helps them to vomit when they must. While cats sometimes chew house plants, outside it is very rare for them to eat plants that might be harmful to them, as there are so many other distractions.

catnip

One plant that many cats find hard to ignore outdoors is *Nepeta cataria*, or catnip. This has an amazing effect on many cats — they drool at the smell of it and roll and rub themselves in it to cover themselves with its scent. Thankfully, this is completely harmless.

Cats love chasing insects that fly near open water and watching fish that swim in it.

Chemicals

Unfortunately, kittens are often attracted to the insides of garages and sheds, where they can find chemicals and other things that are harmful if eaten. Anti-freeze is particularly dangerous. Take your kitten to the veterinarian if you suspect that he has eaten or drank something that may be a risk to his health.

Other cats

Cats are very territorial creatures. This means they will defend their yard or an area that

Toads look like fun to a kitten, but the skin tastes horrible and makes the cat dribble.

Kittens can find lots of things to see and do in the yard. Playing with leaves is a favorite.

Occasionally, kittens find frogs or toads in the yard and cannot resist playing with them. Some toads have a nasty coating on their skin that hurts an animal's mouth if it tries to bite its prize, making it foam around the mouth. Call your veterinarian if you think that your kitten has been playing with something he shouldn't!

In some areas, venomous snakes and other animals may be a risk to your kitten's life; on a visit to your veterinarian, ask if there any dangerous creatures living nearby you should know about.

they think of as their own. Although most cats would rather run than fight, neighboring cats sometimes get into fights. If you think your kitten has been in a fight, check him over very carefully or take him to the veterinarian for a thorough examination.

Other animals

Your kitten might get stung by a wasp or bee. Although this is painful, it probably won't cause a problem — and it means that the cat will be more careful next time!

Cats are very agile and have excellent balance, so climbing trees and walking along narrow things, like the top of a fence or a branch, is easy.

walking on a harness and leash

Some owners teach their cat to walk on a harness and leash, because it is not safe to let the cat outside on his own, or because the owners want to travel with him. Teaching a cat to walk on a leash is more difficult than teaching a puppy the same thing. Most cats enjoy their freedom, so they don't like being on the end of a leash, where they can't run away if they wish.

Harness training needs to be started when the kitten is very young. You will need lots of patience if you are to succeed. Choose a harness that suits your kitten's shape and size, with straps that can be altered as your kitten grows up. The edges of the harness should be smooth and soft, so they don't hurt or rub the cat.

Before you try walking your kitten on a leash, make sure that he is completely comfortable wearing the harness on its own.

Lots of leash-walking practice should be done indoors, before going outside where there are sights, smells, and sounds that could scare a cat.

1. Put the harness on your kitten, being very careful not to frighten him. If he struggles and tries to run away, ask an adult to help you, or put it on him while he is distracted by food.

2. Spend a lot of time making sure that your kitten is comfortable and happy wearing the harness before you attach the leash or line. Put the harness on your kitten before feeding him, playing with him, and spending time stroking him, for a few minutes each time. He will then think of wearing the harness as something rewarding.

Cats love being free to explore outdoors, but make sure it is safe for your kitten before letting him out.

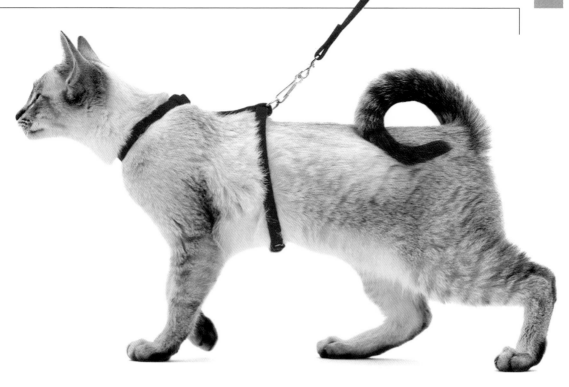

Training your cat to walk on a harness and leash takes a lot of time and patience.

3. Over a few days, leave the harness on the kitten for longer periods while he is in the home and you are there to watch him. When he is completely relaxed about wearing it, attach a piece of very light cord or string to the harness, so that the kitten can get used to the feel of having something attached to it.

4. Gently hold the end of the cord, but allow your kitten to go wherever he wants. Do not pull the cord. If the kitten starts to move away, drop the cord or follow him. Never pull the cord or allow the kitten to play with the end of the cord, or walking him on the harness will be almost impossible later on.

5. When your kitten is happy to walk on the harness and cord, switch the cord for a light leash or a long, lightweight line. Practice in short, fun sessions, walking around the home.

6. When your kitten is totally relaxed about wearing the harness and leash, go out into the yard. Again, take things slowly and allow the kitten to explore and become familiar with the new smells, sights, and sounds. Follow him around rather than trying to guide him.

Although there are dangers to allowing your kitten outside, cats soon learn to keep out of trouble. The joy that kittens and cats have playing, running, leaping, and climbing outdoors is a large part of their life, and allows them to use all of their natural instincts.

3 other cat activities

showing your cat

For some owners, admiring their own cat is not enough — they want to show off its beauty to others as well! Cat shows are held across the world and are not only for purebred cats of distinct breeds. Smaller, local shows often hold contests for non-purebred cats and these can be just as fun as the bigger, more competitive shows.

If you are planning to show your cat, it is important that he is very used to being handled and is confident in all situations. At most of the larger shows, cats are required to be housed in show pens, where the public can walk past and view them. This is very scary for a cat that is not used to meeting so many strangers.

above: *This purebred kitten is a potential champion, but every cat deserves to have its photograph taken!*

Show cats are also picked up and handled by the judges. This is usually done when the cat's owner is not around, so your kitten will have to be really happy about meeting strangers.

To find out when and where cat shows will be held, look for advertisements in cat magazines or posters and leaflets in veterinary hospitals and pet stores. You will probably need to send off for an entry form and follow a schedule that tells you the show's rules and regulations and lists all the types of contest so you know which one to enter.

The preparation you need to do before the show depends on the type of coat your kitten

The bustle and excitement of a cat show, owners, visitors, and judges viewing the cats in their fancy cages.

has. Grooming is essential for all breeds and types, so that the cat is free of dirt and the fur is not matted but shines with health. If you own one of the longhaired breeds, bathing and many hours of grooming will be needed if your cat is to look his best.

Winners at cat shows usually receive rosettes or prizes. The overall winner is classed as "Best In Show." It is very exciting to win an award at a cat show, but don't be downhearted if you don't win anything — after all, you are lucky enough to be taking the very best cat home!

agility test

Some cats have been trained go over small obstacle courses! If you want to test your kitten's agility, start by placing a pole on the floor and teaching him to step over it by luring him with a tasty treat or a toy. Raise the pole a little each time, so that he has to jump higher. Once your kitten has mastered the high jump, create new obstacles for him. Try teaching him to climb a small ramp or run through a tunnel made from cardboard boxes.

cats on film

Taking photographs of your kitten can be difficult, as cats are very wriggly and fast-moving. If you can train your cat to sit still (*see page 70*), you can take close-up pictures of his face to show his different expressions.

You can test your kittens' agility with simple home-made obstacle, like this tunnel made from the leg of some pants.

Don't forget that action pictures are great fun, too! See if you can catch your kitten stalking, running, or jumping. His days as a small, cute kitten won't last long, and the photographs will be a wonderful reminder of those days.

Some very well-trained cats don't just pose for photographs, they also perform for movies and TV. Cats need to be very confident to be able to cope with all the hustle and bustle of a film studio, with cameras pointing at them, lights blazing, and lots of movement and sounds from the movie-makers. If your kitten looks and acts like a film or TV star, use a video camera to record his best tricks, and then send the tape to an animal acting agency — ask an adult to find the address for you. If they think he could be a star, the agency will tell you what you need to do next to get your cat up on the screen.

conclusion

In past times, people used to rely on cats to hunt mice to protect stores of food. Now, we love them for the affection and fun that they bring. Although they live in our homes, eat the food we give them, and sit on our laps, they are still wild at heart. This is part of what makes kittens and cats such interesting pets.

Kittens are full of fun, energy, and mischief. They are playful and affectionate. But the cute, fluffy stage does not last for long — soon your kitten will have grown into a graceful, athletic adult cat. She will still enjoy your company and want to play, but she will be independent and lead a life of her own, parts of which will be a mystery to you!

In their first few weeks of life, kittens learn about people and the way that we live. They discover that humans provide food, shelter, and love, and they form strong friendships with us in return, which often last for life. Cats are happy to curl up with us on the couch when we are sad, or play exciting games when we are want some fun; they are very good at understanding our moods. Using this book to learn about cats and the meaning of your kitten's body language and expressions will allow you to understand her moods too, and will prove that you don't need to speak to tell someone something!

Kittens turn into cats very quickly. Enjoy the time you have with your kitten — growing up together will be fun for both of you!